Ken

## A GUIDE TO
## BASIC CHRISTIAN BELIEFS

# YOU'D
# BETTER
# BELIEVE
# IT!

GOSPEL PUBLISHING HOUSE
SPRINGFIELD, MISSOURI
02-0887

YOU'D BETTER BELIEVE IT!
© 1975 by the Gospel Publishing House, Springfield, Missouri 65802. All rights reserved. Adapted from *The Fundamentals of the Faith* by Donald Johns, © 1963 by the Gospel Publishing House. Library of Congress Catalog Card No. 75-22608. Printed in the United States of America. ISBN 0-88243-887-5.

A teacher's guide for group study with this book is available from the Gospel Publishing House (order no. 32-0161).

# Contents

# 1
# We're in Big Trouble

### WHO SAYS SO?

"This is the Internal Revenue Service. Have you filed an income tax return for last year?" The voice on the telephone proved to be that of a friend having his day's fun, though for one anxious moment I thought Uncle Sam had his spotlight on me.

But this is no joke. We're in big trouble; all of us. Who says so? God! Maybe you've been hearing that all we need is an improvement in our ecology, an upgrading of our education, a redistribution of our wealth. Too many do-gooders try to make us think it's the outside of us that needs overhauling. But even without any Bible knowledge there's an uneasy feeling inside us that such propaganda is phony.

Our big mess started on the inside. "All have sinned!" (Romans 3:23). Wham! That hurts, doesn't it? Pride takes a licking when we start talking about sin and guilt and depravity. Better watch it! Pride can be like a rock tied around a man's neck when he's in 10 feet of water and can't swim in the first place. He keeps going under, but won't jerk the rock off.

If it's any comfort, we're all in the same boat. God leaves no one out—the rich, the poor, the white, the black, the brown, the man with the white collar and the one with the blue collar. We may not all move in the same social circles, but spiritually we are at the bottom of the same well. That word is short, but it's powerful: "All!"

When I rushed off to a tornado shelter in the middle of the night a few years ago I had lots of company. They were of all ages. Whether their salary was more than mine or less concerned me not a bit. We were all in the same boat—or shelter, in this case. A safe spot was what we needed, and we had found it.

So don't strut like a peacock and say "sinner" is a mark the Lord might put on some people but not on you!

That verse had a big finger pointing right out of the middle of it, and it's God's. No matter where you run or hide, there it is—aimed right at your heart. "All have sinned." It's not a pretty tune to hear, but it's what troubles the human race.

"Cancer" isn't a pretty word either, but it does no good to pretend you don't have it when you do.

Some people are afraid to go to the doctor for fear of what his dagnosis will be. Maybe that's why so many don't want to get any nearer God than they can help. The Lord is no killjoy. But He can't heal you until you know how sick you are. So He puts it in plain, blunt language that a child can understand.

A SEED THAT ALWAYS SPROUTS

Some people can put a stick in the ground and it will bloom. I am not one of that breed. I plant things that never grow. If they come up they just don't last long. No green thumb!

The Bible has much to say about a seed that always sprouts. It grows, and grows, and never stops.

Let's get its name right out in the open. There is no use beating around the bush. The seed is "sin."

We don't become sinners accidentally. The seed lies in the soil of our innermost being when we come into this world, and only waits the passing of time to show its ugly head. God says so. "But I was born a sinner, yes, from the moment my mother conceived me" (Psalm 51:5, *Living Bible Paraphrased*).

The first man, Adam, became a sinner because he let the devil hoodwink him into disobeying the Lord's plain orders. It was a tragedy from which the race has never recovered.

Physically we pass characteristics from generation to generation. Tendencies toward certain diseases can be inherited. This is what hit the human family when Adam fell into Satan's snare. Ever since that catastrophe the seed of sin has been in every man.

This seed needs no special climate or care. It grows in the home of the rich and poor. It springs up in the son of the atheist and the child of the devout man.

Would you like to hear more? "There is none righteous, no, not one" (Romans 3:10). How plain can God get. Is He trying to humiliate us? No, just laboring to show us how fouled up we are on the inside of ourselves so we'll stop trying to paint and plaster the outside.

Can you picture yourself as an old reprobate dressed in tattered, dirty clothes? Maybe not, but God sees the inside of you and me and every one of our fellow humans just like this. Listen: "But we are all as an unclean thing, and all our righteousnesses are as filthy rags" (Isaiah 64:6).

This is quite a blow to the man who gloats over his clean record. He thinks his churchgoing, debtpaying and honorable living make him look like a king. God says, "The more of that stuff you try to impress Me with, the more you remind Me of a bum!"

In that same verse the writer bemoans that "we all do fade as a leaf; and our iniquities, like the wind, have taken us away." That's a different figure, but a plain one. Every one is like a dead leaf clinging to the tree of self-righteousness, but ready to be blown away at any moment by the strong wind of sin.

Maybe your gardening experience is like mine. Your seeds may never sprout, but if you don't deal with that sin on the inside of you it's going to cause you misery forever.

## An Unsealed Indictment

Grand juries sometimes indict people but keep the names secret until the arrests are made. These unsealed indictments are a necessary part of our legal process. How would you feel if there was a chance one of the names was yours?

An indictment has been handed down by the great Judge in heaven. It covers the whole human race, and He makes no effort to cover it up. It's there for each one to see: "No one has ever really followed God's paths, or even truly wanted to. Every one has turned away; all have gone wrong. No one anywhere has kept on doing what is right; not one" (Romans 3:11,12, *Living Bible Paraphrased*).

Is God trying to add insult to injury? Does He keep pouring it on just to show us how much contempt He has for man? Far from it. Let's establish once and for all that God desperately wants to rescue us. He is not happy over our plight. He alone can get us out of it.

But what does He encounter when He tries to reach us? One roadblock after another. We turn deaf ears. We show Him our backs. We don't think we

8

need Him. Life hasn't got so tough that *we* can't handle it!

So the Lord has to hit us hard. It's the only way He can get our attention. Soft words don't make us even blink.

If we think there is any possible way of earning our own way to heaven we'll try it. So a loving Father has to knock every last prop out from under us. He must slam some of us with the Truth in so many difrent ways that we finally wake up and admit, "I guess I really am lost!"

No one is going to hire a defense attorney if he doesn't know he has been accused of something. Neither is a man going to fly to the arms of Jesus if he doesn't realize he is under indictment for crimes that will bring the death sentence down on his head.

God has His hardest time getting through to the "good moral man." The sot in the gutter knows he needs a helping hand, but not Mr. Big! One of this kind paid a night visit to Jesus. His name was Nicodemus, and he was a very "religious" man. What did our Lord tell him? "You can't even *see* inside the kingdom of heaven in your present state!"

We have come a long way since the horse-and-buggy days. Jets scream through the skies, and spaceships hurtle toward the planets. There is instant communication from one part of the globe to another. But none of this touches the spot where all trouble starts—the individual human heart. Change that heart, and you will eliminate war, poverty, crime, and all of the other miserable side effects of sin.

Plead innocent all you like, but the indictment is there. And you and I can't erase it.

### YES, IT'S TERMINAL

Many a pastor has had someone follow him out of

a hospital room to tell him, away from the patient's hearing, "The doctor says it's terminal." What a blow! How final!

We are constantly warned to keep a close watch on our physical condition so that diseases, if any develop, can be detected in their early stages. Unfortunately some do not manifest themselves until it is too late to treat them.

Sin, if it is not dealt with, is a terminal disease. It will not get better. Its hold only grows more tenacious.

We have other names for sin now. Sometimes we are even told it does not exist. But this is only wishful thinking, propagated by those who are themselves victims of the terminal disease.

"The wages of sin is death" (Romans 6:23). That's God's diagnosis, and if we're smart we'll listen. We outgrow some things with the passing of the years, but not sin. It may take on more respectable forms as we get older and want to improve our image, but it's still there.

Never think that because your conscience isn't burning you up every minute you are in no spiritual danger. You can try to silence your conscience and ignore it, but you will still have to face judgment some day.

The worst sins are those the world doesn't see. They are buried deep within us, but they have a vicious grip. Selfishness, hatred, greed, lust, and a host of other sins are like malignant cells spreading wildly to every part of our being. Our deeds of charity can't destroy them. They are like the spreading leprosy so common in Bible times.

This disease called "sin" destroys the finest qualities in a man. Worst of all, it strangles his ability to know God.

10

Sin keeps us on the animal level. The beast may be concealed under a lot of sophistication, but it is still there.

Some maladies that take a man's life can be so insidious that he may feel perfectly well one week and be dead the next. Sin is just this subtle. It kills while a person thinks he is doing fine. He is not conscious that the very fabric of his personality is being eroded; that his spiritual sensibilities are disappearing. Slowly, but surely, he is dying on the inside. A Christian friend may express concern, but the victim only smiles and assures him his worries are unnecessary. He may compliment the minister on his sermon, while smugly congratulating himself that it doesn't apply to him.

## DON'T BLAME THE SYSTEM!

"The devil made me do it!" Isn't it amazing how fast that little line spread after Flip Wilson came up with it on TV. I wonder why? Is it because everyone is looking for someone to blame for his wrongdoing —even if it is the devil?

Of course the most recent scapegoat is "the system," or "the establishment," as some call it. There are actually people who don t believe in any type of punishment for crime because it is all the fault of the system, they declare.

It is very comfortable to excuse ourselves for violating God's laws because of something our parents did, or didn't do. Maybe it's the schoolteacher, the police, the boss, our wife, or husband. But never us!

It may come as a surprise, but God says He will hold each of us individually responsible for our deeds. Adam sinned because he chose to listen to Satan instead of God. The devil can't *make* you do *any*thing.

11

He can offer strong inducements, but the final choice is yours.

When you're in the voting booth you are the only one who can pull the lever on that machine. The same is true with every other decision in your life.

"So then every one of us shall give account of himself to God" (Romans 14:12). Read that verse again and be sure to underline "himself."

A young man in the Old Testament named Daniel was taken to heathen Babylon and ordered to violate God's laws by eating the king's meat and drinking his wine. Others were following orders meekly, but the Bible says, "Daniel purposed in his heart that he would not defile himself" (Daniel 1:8). And he didn't. The choice was his, and he made the right one —just as you and I can.

Of course, the right road is never easy. Floating downstream is the way of least resistance. But many a man has bucked the current. If you say someone else is to blame for your spiritual condition you're employing a well-worn cop-out.

There is one thing God has given to every man equally, and that is a free will. That's why He didn't stop Adam from sinning. God didn't want a robot. He wanted a man who would serve Him because He wanted to; not because he couldn't do otherwise.

You can use that free will to obey God or to disobey Him. The Bible says that every man, without exception, has used it to disobey. If we would find our way out of our dilemma we must not say, "It wasn't my fault. I was forced into it." You are not a piece of driftwood being tossed about by a capricious sea. You are a human being with the awesome capability of choice.

## The Bottom of the Hill

I was raised where it snowed a lot in winter. Close to my school was a hill that became very slippery during those cold months. Many of us had sleds that we often brought to school. Recesses and noon hours were spent speeding down that hill. Faster and faster we went until it seemed we might take off. Of course the fun was over when we reached the bottom.

Life away from God reminds me of that icy hill. At first we don't go so fast, but the farther we travel the more our momentum increases. It's fun now, but what will it be like when it's all over?

The Bible says that if a man dies lost he will stay lost forever. It is like cement that finally sets until its permanent form is determined.

"It is appointed unto men once to die, but after this the judgment" (Hebrews 9:27). That sounds very final, doesn't it? No second chance. No opportunity to go back and make changes. We have written our last chapter.

It is hard for us to realize what is it like to be cut off from God forever—which is what it means to be lost. God lets us have a little glimpse of that future trial when all men who have lived and died without Him receive their final sentence. Here it is:

"And I saw a great white throne and the one who sat upon it, from whose face the earth and sky fled away, but they found no place to hide. I saw the dead, great and small, standing before God; and The Books were opened, including the Book of Life. And the dead were judged according to the things written in The Books, each according to the deeds he had done. The oceans surrendered the bodies buried in them; and the earth and the underworld gave up the dead in them. Each was judged according to his deeds. And Death and Hell were thrown into the Lake of Fire. This is the Second Death—the Lake of Fire. And if anyone's name was not found recorded in the Book of Life, he was thrown into the Lake of Fire" (Revelation 20:11-15, *Living Bible Paraphrased*).

Not a pretty picture, is it? But God says it will be this way if we turn our backs on Him and keep going. It's what it will be like at the bottom of the hill. Lots of fun on the way down, wasn't it? But now the fun is over. The party has ended.

## Would God Really Do This?

A loving God would never send a soul to hell! Sounds convincing, doesn't it? Unfortunately, the reasoning is twisted.

To be sure, God does not send anyone to hell. A man sends himself there by deliberate rebellion. He goes in spite of everything God has done to save him.

If the highway department put up roadblocks and signs warning of a washed-out bridge, and some driver deliberately ignored everything and plunged to his death, who is to blame? Would you condemn the state and say they killed the man?

Our Heavenly Father sent His Son to die on the Cross for our sins. That Cross, like a great barricade, lies across the path of every man. Some rush on to a dark eternity in spite of it. They trample divine love under foot and seal their destiny with their own disobedience.

If God did not carry out the death sentence on those who rebel against Him He would become a prisoner in His own universe. It would be like having

14

a police force that never arrested anyone. The community would shortly become a madhouse. There can be no order unless law is enforced, and this applies to the laws of God.

Be assured that God takes no satisfaction in the damnation of anyone. He says so. He couldn't make it any plainer than He does in Ezekiel 33:11. "As I live, saith the Lord God, I have no pleasure in the death of the wicked; but that the wicked turn from his way and live."

All have sinned. There are eternal consequences for sin. Is there a way out? Indeed there is, and we'll talk about it in the next chapter.

## 2

# Who's That Running Down the Road?

### BACK FROM A LONG TRIP

Wouldn't you have a few questions if you saw an elderly neighbor running down the street as fast as his legs would carry him? What do you suppose the neighbors of the Prodigal Son's father thought when they saw him raising a cloud of dust? They had watched him at the gate day after day, gazing into the distance. No one had to ask what he was looking for. They all noticed how easily he cried after his youngest boy took off for the "far country."

But one day it happened. A figure showed up in the distance. The old man didn't need to look twice. He hadn't run like this since he was a boy, but there he goes!

Can't you imagine a newcomer to the neighborhood shouting to a passerby, "Who's that running down the road?"

This was a story Jesus told to help us realize how much God wants all of us prodigals back home. Like this son of old, we have been off on a long trip to the far country where God is forgotten. The Father has never been too busy guiding the universe to look anxiously for our return.

When you stop to think of it, this is quite a picture for Jesus to paint of God: A man so excited that he throws dignity to the winds and unashamedly dashes pell-mell down the trail to throw his arms around the neck of a boy who has made a mess of his life. But that's the way God feels, Jesus declared. He said the angels even feel it: "There is joy in the presence of the angels of God over one sinner that repenteth" (Luke 15:10).

Lots of prodigals come back home around a church altar, but it doesn't have to happen there. God will take a man back any time he's ready. The Lord is *always* ready—don't forget that. "For whosoever shall call upon the name of the Lord shall be saved" (Romans 10:13).

It doesn't take a genius to "call." If you're in trouble nobody has to teach you how to call for help. God isn't listening for big words and flowery phrases. He knows when a cry is coming from the heart. And what comes from man's heart touches God's heart.

You've been in that far country too long. The trip back isn't nearly as hard as you think.

THERE'S ANOTHER SIDE

Here's something you'll never see: An indictment for a crime with an offer of pardon on the other side.

But if you'll read the Bible that's exactly what you will find. All have sinned. All are equally guilty. All have been indicted. But the same Judge who indicts wants to save.

If you don't believe this, get a Bible and open it to the third chapter of Romans—the passage we focused on in chapter 1. Verse 23 indicts us all: "For all have sinned, and come short of the glory of God." But the very next verse is the offer of pardon: "Being justified freely by his grace through the redemption that is in Christ Jesus." If this seems too good to be true, read it again. It's no dream!

That verse mentions two terms that may seem very theological at first. But really there's nothing so mysterious about them. The first word is "justified." It simply means "to be accounted or declared righteous." Where most of us get mixed up is in trying to be righteous without God's help. *He* says it happens by His grace. Then it's a gift? Exactly.

The second word is "redemption." When you redeem something you buy it back. This is exactly why Jesus died on the Cross. Mankind was lost to God through sin. He created us, but we slipped out of His grasp when we listened to the devil. The only way He could get us back was for a price to be paid. Since none of us could pay the price ourselves, Jesus did it.

God couldn't just forget our sin, or act as though it didn't exist. He had to punish it in order to be just, and when Jesus went to the Cross that's what God did. He punished His innocent Son for sins *we* committed. You are absolutely right if you say, "That means Jesus was my Substitute."

This is how God could write an offer of pardon on the other side of the indictment. What we couldn't possibly do, Jesus did for us.

You are also correct if you refer to Jesus' death as the "atonement" for our sins. God couldn't be satisfied with anything we could do to try to make up for our disobedience. But with Jesus' work on Calvary He is perfectly satisfied. Nothing has to be added to it. No good works, church-joining, or worthy deeds have to be piled on top of the atonement of Jesus. It is enough by itself.

"For God sent Christ Jesus to take the punishment for our sins and to end all God's anger against us. He used Christ's blood and our faith as the means of saving us from his wrath. In this way he was being entirely fair, even though he did not punish those who sinned in former times. For he was looking forward to the time when Christ would come and take away those sins" (Romans 3:25, *Living Bible Paraphrased*).

## A Door With Two Signs

Ever go roaming through a building, looking for a room you couldn't find? It would have been a lot easier if someone hadn't removed the sign from the door, wouldn't it?

It would be no exaggeration to say that everyone who finds God must open the door that says "Repentance" on the outside. This isn't the most pleasant word in the world. It may involve some pretty bad feelings at first. When you wake up to the fact that you are guilty of something it doesn't make you feel like shouting. The Bible says "The Lord is . . . not willing that any should perish, but that all should come to repentance" (2 Peter 3:9). It is through repentance that perishing is avoided. So it's worth all the bad feeling, wouldn't you say?

What is repentance? It's far more than being sorry you got caught! Actually it means "a change of mind." To receive the salvation God has offered, we must change our mind about sin. We must look at sin as God sees it. Naturally this means to detest it; to loathe it; to turn our back on it permanently.

As much as we may shrink from that "Repentance" sign, when we once open the door we'll find another sign on the inside. It's a welcome one. It says "Salvation." But you never see the second sign until you open the door.

If you want to keep on with this picture, you would be right in saying that the knob on the door is "Faith." This is what enables us to open the door. It's hard to do much with a door whose knob has vanished.

Something else ought to be said about faith. If it's only skull deep you'll never get the door open. It must be deep enough to result in a commitment. You don't get into God's family by saying, "I'll try this for a while and see if it works." You have to be like a man who crosses a river and never looks back.

The kind of faith that saves is not based on feelings. That's like basing it on the weather—too many changes. The only safe foundation for our faith is the Word of God. If you can't trust *God's* Word, who *can* you trust?

This is one door that's easy to find. The sign has never been removed. Get your blinders off. It's right there in front of you!

Since we have been talking about a door, let's stay with that picture a moment longer. When you open the door of "Salvation" you don't step into a vacuum or a dark hallway. That door leads into a large, bright room called "Regeneration."

There's another word that seems like a jawbreaker. You may be more familiar with the expression, "the new birth." They mean the same. When you regenerate something you create it again. When you repent and turn to Christ in faith, He creates *you* again. He gives you a new birth. It's a new beginning!

Let's go to the highest authority—Jesus Christ—and hear His explanation: "Men can only reproduce human life, but the Holy Spirit gives new life from heaven; so don't be surprised at my statement that you must be born again! Just as you can hear the wind but can't tell where it comes from or where it will go next, so it is with the Spirit. We do not know on whom he will next bestow this life from heaven" (John 3:6-8, *Living Bible Paraphrased*).

The Bible goes so far as to say that a man away from God is dead. Spiritually dead, that is. He may be alive physically, but the part of him that should be responding to God is dead. The new birth Jesus talks about makes us spiritually alive as children of the Heavenly Father. God no longer views us as guilty of sin. He says we are righteous because we have accepted Christ as our Saviour and have inherited *His* righteousness.

God offers the same salvation to every person. Everyone must receive it in the same way. There is nothing complicated about His plan of redeeming us. A child can understand it. Instead of putting salvation on a shelf so high no one can reach it, the Lord has put it where everyone can if they will.

Repentance, faith, regeneration—these aren't really hard to comprehend when you really want to find the way to God. A fresh start; a clean slate—wouldn't it be great! It *is* great, and it's just what happens when we open the door of repentance.

### Better Than Your Own Name

If you handed me a check and said, "Here's a little gift for you," the first thing I would look for would be my name on it.

There's a word that pops up in the Bible pretty often, and it's even better than seeing your own name. The word is "whosoever." Remember that verse in the beginning of this chapter? "For whosoever shall call upon the name of the Lord shall be saved."

And who doesn't know John 3:16: "For God so loved the world that he gave his only begotten Son, that whosoever believeth in him should not perish, but have everlasting life."

21

If verses like this had your name in them it would exclude everyone else. And how could you be sure it didn't mean someone else with the same name? But "whosoever"—that's like a blank check. It puts everybody on the same level. God plays no favorites, and He shuts nobody out.

The Lord wants everyone to be saved. He wants everyone to repent, to believe, to be regenerated. This is why Jesus pictured God in the parable as a man running excitedly down the road to meet a wayward son. Saving your soul is no routine matter with God. It involves His very heart!

When God looks down He doesn't see a forest. He sees trees—not a mass of humanity, but you, and you, and you. He made us all a little different. Each one is unique, and each one matters to Him. We all have the same basic need—salvation. Just as we are born individually and die individually, so we are saved one at a time. The salvation of each man is an important transaction as far as heaven is concerned.

"If any man be in Christ, he is a new creature" (2 Corinthians 5:17). There's that individual emphasis again: "any man."

Sheep and shepherds were everywhere in Jesus' day, so He used them to help us comprehend the value God puts on one soul. We might think a shepherd who has all of his sheep but one safely inside the fold would lie down by the fire for a good night's sleep. What is one sheep when there are ninety-nine bedded down safe and sound?

That's not the way a shepherd's heart works, Jesus said. There is no rest for him until he has found the one lost sheep. It is inconvenient and tiring. He leaves a warm bed. The night is dark and stormy. There is danger. But he doesn't stop until the lost is found.

And how does he treat the sheep he finds? Scold it for being lost? On the contrary, "He layeth it on his shoulders," Jesus declared (Luke 15:5). The poor animal is exhausted from its wandering, so the shepherd doesn't make it suffer anymore. Only when he can put it down in its own bed does he take the sheep off his own strong shoulders.

## THE LONGEST WORD

What is the longest word in the English language? I haven't checked the dictionary lately, so I can't tell you for sure.

But, laying aside the mere counting of letters, I would say that the longest word is "saved." Just five letters, to be sure, but it's what the word contains that counts.

If a man were pardoned a few moments before he went to the gallows his first cause for rejoicing would be the deliverance from death. It is natural that a Christian thanks God first of all that he is delivered from sin's guilt and penalty. He was indicted, but now is pardoned. He was guilty, but now is righteous.

This is only the beginning. When we are regenerated, or born again, we are also delivered from sin's power.

Let's face it, we weren't really our own boss when we were away from God. There is nothing independent about a life of sin. We were slaves, and Satan was our master. We thought we were guiding our lives, but he was influencing our decisions all the time.

Every New Year's Day we made noble resolutions, and we really meant them. But most of them didn't last one day. Frustration built up to the point of explosion because we were always doing things we really wanted to stop doing.

The new birth changes this. We are still not our own boss, but we are not under the old one any longer. God is in command now. We are able to get loose from those old habits. No longer do we feel like a sailboat being driven by the wind. We are more like a car moving down the highway with God at the steering wheel.

Salvation means access to God. It means having the Holy Spirit as our Teacher. It means divine light on our pathway. And it's all by His grace, not our works.

### ALL THIS AND HEAVEN, TOO?

"Pie in the sky when you die." That's the way some skeptics describe the Christian's hope. How little they know!

We don't go to heaven the next minute after we are saved. For many there are years and years of living on earth. This means grappling with problems, enduring tough times, shedding tears, getting sick, and a lot of other things. It also means having a lot of happiness. There will be roses as well as thorns.

The glory of the gospel is that it enables a man to live in this present world and stay on top of the situation. No one ever put it better than Paul: "Godliness is profitable unto all things, having promise of the life that now is, and of that which is to come" (1 Timothy 4:8).

Of course, life comes to an end. The final reward of a Christian is not on this earth. It is eternal fellowship with God in heaven.

The human heart yearns for heaven. An instinctive desire for heaven seems to be implanted within the heart of every human. Regardless of his culture or race, man longs for a place after death where all is joy and happiness.

The Bible tells us that such a place exists. John, banished to the Isle of Patmos, had a vision of the eternal land he was soon to enter. This vision, found in portions of Revelation 21 and 22, gives us one of the most detailed descriptions of heaven. Read it the first chance you have.

If you think salvation isn't for you, think of that father running down the road, oblivious of everything else but the lone figure trudging up the path. That father is a picture of God, Jesus said. And the returning son can be a picture of you!

# 3
# *Let the Whole World Know*

The Christian life is basically one of obedience. Sometimes it's easier to obey the big commandments than the small ones. But an order from the Lord is an order, be it large or small.

A child doesn't run a 100-yard dash the first time it manages a step. We walk before we run, and walking itself begins a step at a time. The Christian life is very much the same. If we take one small step of obedience it makes the next one easier. Steps make a walk, and a walk makes a life.

One of the first steps Christians must take is that of water baptism. This is what we'll be talking about in this chapter, and it's no small matter. Even if you think you know all about the subject, lend an ear. Spiritual truths bear a lot of repeating.

## IT'S NOT AN OPTION

Who said we "must"? Jesus himself. Listen: "Go ye therefore, and teach all nations, baptizing them in the name of the Father, and of the Son, and of the Holy Ghost, teaching them to observe all things whatsoever I have commanded you: and, lo, I am with you alway, even unto the end of the world. Amen" (Matthew 28:19,20).

Historically, Protestants have recognized the existence of two ordinances of the Church: The Lord's Supper, and water baptism. What does "ordinance" mean? In its broadest sense it simply means a "thing commanded or ordained."

Jesus didn't waste words. It was just before His ascension that He instructed His apostles to practice and teach water baptism. At such a time He would speak only of things He considered most vital. Water baptism, then, must be one of those things.

Let's talk for a moment about John's baptism. Although the method was the same, its meaning was different than Christian baptism. Paul found some of John's followers at Ephesus who had not even heard of the Holy Spirit. They had been baptized by John, but were rebaptized by Paul after he explained the gospel to them (Acts 19:1-7). Had Christian baptism been the same as John's, there would have been no reason for this second baptism.

The baptism of John was a baptism of repentance (Acts 19:4; Matthew 3:11; Mark 1:4; Luke 3:3). It symbolized, or represented, repentance that was sincere. When an individual let John baptize him he was saying by this act that he believed the Messiah was coming. In preparation for that coming he was repenting of his sins, and proclaiming it to the world by being baptized (Mark 1:7; Luke 3:16; John 1:27).

Christians do not look forward to the Messiah's coming, for He has already come. We look *back*—to the Cross, to the open tomb, and to our Lord's ascension.

### WE'RE IN GOOD COMPANY

The first baptismal service in the church was a big one. Have you ever seen 3,000 baptized on the same day? It happened on the Day of Pentecost. Listen to Peter's altar call, and what followed:

"Then Peter said unto them, Repent, and be baptized every one of you in the name of Jesus Christ for the remission of sins, and ye shall receive the gift of the Holy Ghost. For the promise is unto you, and to your children, and to all that are afar off, even as many as the Lord our God shall call. And with many other words did he testify and exhort, saying, Save yourselves from this untoward generation. Then they that gladly received his word were baptized: and the same day there were added unto them about three thousand souls" (Acts 2:38-41).

No one should be baptized just to be observing a ritual. The order of events at Pentecost was exactly the way it should always be. Peter preached, and those who heard the sermon were "pricked in their heart" (Acts 2:37). When they asked what they should do, Peter told them to repent and be baptized. That's what they did. First, they heard the Word and felt convicted for their sins. Then they repented and publicly declared their experience by being baptized.

Other baptismal services are recorded in the Book of Acts. Philip baptized the Ethiopian eunuch (Acts 8:36-38). This happened immediately after the man declared his faith in Christ. Paul was baptized at Damascus soon after his conversion (Acts 9:18). Paul himself baptized converts. One of the nost notable occasions was the baptism of the Philippian jailer (Acts 16:33). Before this Paul baptized Lydia and her household (Acts 16:15).

Paul preached at Corinth a year and a half, and continued his practice of baptizing converts (Acts 18:8-11). He specially mentioned baptizing Crispus,

Gaius, and the household of Stephanas (1 Corinthians 1:14-16).

Peter ordered the baptism of the Gentiles who accepted Christ at Caesarea (Acts 10:47,48).

The practice of baptism in water by the apostles and the Early Church indicates how important it was as a fulfillment of the command of Jesus. Don't shrink from baptism. It's a privilege as well as a duty for one who has been truly converted.

## HERE'S THE PICTURE

The Bible is full of pictures that help us understand spiritual truths. That's why Jesus taught in parables. He took something that people easily understood and used it to illustrate something that was harder to grasp.

Baptism in water is a picture of a spiritual truth. There is a passage in Romans that emphasizes this very strongly. It's long, but worth reading in its entirety. Here it is:

"Well then, shall we keep on sinning so that God can keep on showing us more and more kindness and forgiveness?

"Of course not! Should we keep on sinning when we don't have to? For sin's power over us was broken when we became Christians and were baptized to become a part of Jesus Christ; through his death the power of your sinful nature was shattered. Your old sin-loving nature was buried with him by baptism when he died, and when God the Father, with glorious power, brought him back to life again, you were given his wonderful new life to enjoy.

"For you have become a part of him, and so you died with him, so to speak, when he died; and now you share his new life, and shall rise as he did. Your old evil desires were nailed to the cross with him;

29

that part of you that loves to sin was crushed and fatally wounded, so that your sin-loving body is no longer under sin's control, no longer needs to be a slave to sin; for when you are deadened to sin you are freed from all its allure and its power over you. And since your old sin-loving nature 'died' with Christ, we know that you will share his new life. Christ rose from the dead and will never die again. Death no longer has any power over him. He died once for all to end sin's power, but now he lives forever in unbroken fellowship with God. So look upon your old sin nature as dead and unresponsive to sin, and instead be alive to God, alert to him, through Jesus Christ our Lord" (Romans 6:1-11, *Living Bible Paraphrased*).

There you have it. The experience of conversion means that what happened to Christ physically on the Cross happens to our old sinful nature. It dies. But Jesus did not stay dead. He arose. So do we when we are saved. After the old nature dies there is a resurrection, and a new person emerges. We are starting a new life, just as Jesus did when He came out of the tomb.

What better picture could there be of death, burial, and resurrection than going under the water and coming back up again?

## "UP OUT OF THE WATER"

Does it make any difference how you are baptized? Isn't one method as good as another? What about sprinkling or the other means that have been used at times?

Let's forget the opinions of people, or even the ritual of churches. Personal convenience should also be disregarded. What does the Bible itself teach about the mode of baptism?

30

The Greek word for "baptize" means "to dip." Every place it is used in the New Testament it means an immersion. No one needs to hesitate about saying that immersion is the scriptural manner of baptism.

Jesus was baptized "in Jordan." He came "up out of the water" (Mark 1:9,10).

John the Baptist said, "I indeed baptized you in water" (Mark 1:8, literal translation).

Both Philip and the Ethiopian eunuch whom he baptized "went down both into the water" and came "up out of the water" (Acts 8:38,39).

According to the command of Jesus, baptism should be "in the name of the Father, and of the Son, and of the Holy Ghost" (Matthew 28:19). This is a recognition that the Triune Godhead participates in the salvation of men.

Why, then, are there passages in Acts saying that people were baptized in the name of Jesus? (Acts 2:38; 8:16; 19:5). This does not refer to the formula used in baptism. Baptism "in the name of Jesus" was to distinguish it from the baptism of John; to show that it was Christian baptism. Acts 10:48 speaks of those who were baptized "in the name of the Lord." If this referred to the baptismal formula it would indicate that sometimes the apostles baptized in the name of Jesus Christ, sometimes in the name of the Lord Jesus, and also in the name of the Lord. These expressions were simply to distinguish these baptisms from the baptism of John, with which so many were familiar.

Should we not desire to follow the example of Jesus? There is no question that He was immersed. So were the multitudes who followed Him in baptism in Acts. Any other mode of baptism fails to give a picture of what really happens to us when we are

31

saved. Death, burial, and resurrection! What a picture of our Christian experience!

## DOES WATER WASH AWAY OUR SINS?

The obvious answer to this question is an emphatic "No!" Nothing but the blood of Jesus cleanses a sinful soul. To ascribe such powers to anything else is heresy.

To teach that baptism is synonymous with conversion is to sanction "baptismal regeneration." Only the most tortured explanation of Scripture could lead one to believe that baptismal water has some mysterious power to cleanse and regenerate the soul.

Being baptized is a matter of obedience *following* salvation. Only God himself knows how many people have been baptized without an experience of conversion. Naturally they are just as unconverted after their baptism as before.

In Mark 16:16 we read, "He that believeth and is baptized shall be saved; but he that believeth not shall be damned." Some people take the first part of this verse to try to prove baptismal regeneration. Please note, however, that the latter part does not say, "He who does not believe and is not baptized shall be damned." No mention is made of baptism, but of believing, as far as everlasting condemnation is concerned. It is the believing that saves. It should be followed by baptism, but the baptism is not involved in the actual conversion.

Listen to a few statements of Paul concerning people he baptized:

"But did I, Paul, die for your sins? Were any of you baptized in my name? I am so thankful now that I didn't baptize any of you except Crispus and Gaius.

For now no one can think that I have been trying to start something new, beginning a 'Church of Paul.' Oh, yes, and I baptized the family of Stephanas. I don't remember ever baptizing anyone else. For Christ didn't send me to baptize, but to preach the gospel" (1 Corinthians 1:13-17, *Living Bible Paraphrased*).

We have noted a part of this passage before to demonstrate that Paul carried out Christ's command to baptize. We point to the whole passage now to show that the apostle did not baptize because it saved people. Otherwise he would not have said that Christ did not send him primarily to baptize. He said he was even glad he had not baptized too many, since this might have caused some to think he was trying to gather a personal following. If baptism meant salvation he would have baptized everyone regardless of the repercussions against himself.

## LET'S KEEP OUR BALANCE

Advocates of baptismal regeneration like to quote Acts 2:38 as proof that baptism washes away sins. It must be understood, however, that the first thing Peter cried was "Repent!" Being baptized follows repentance. To be baptized "in the name of Jesus" indicates full acceptance of Him as Saviour. This is what cleanses; not the water.

Acts 22:16 is also used by some who attach power to the water, but here is another example of using part of a Scripture passage and not the whole verse: "And now why tarriest thou? arise, and be baptized, and wash away thy sins, calling upon the name of the Lord."

People who are trying to bolster their point on baptismal regeneration stop with "wash away thy sins." They forget to notice that there is a command

33

here, and that the rest of the verse reads, "calling on the name of the Lord." It is this "calling" that delivers us from sin; not the water in which we are immersed.

There is a beautiful balance to all scriptural truth. There is balance in the Bible's teaching on water baptism. It is commanded. This command must be obeyed. It must be observed by all saved people. But it does not cleanse the soul. It is a picture of salvation; a testimony to the world. But it takes the blood of Jesus to make us clean on the inside.

### Everyone's Watching

Being baptized publicly is like burning your bridges behind you and cutting off any path of retreat to the old life. It is unfortunate that some who have been saved put off their baptism so long. You may even have heard people say they are "praying about it." No need for that! God has already given us the answer.

Being baptized does not cost the Christian in America the persecution it does in many foreign countries. Perhaps it would be good if it did.

But even in America people still recognize that baptism identifies an individual with Christ. For this reason we should be positive that there is no question about our salvation. It does no good to "go down a dry sinner and come up a wet one."

Once we have followed the Lord into the waters of baptism we should be very conscious of our responsibility to live in obedience to every other command. Being baptized is not the only way we must obey Him. Every step we take with Christ must be governed by His Word. We are no longer our own. It all started with repentance—just as Peter preached on the Day of Pentecost. And it will end in heaven!

34

# 4
# You Can Be a Winner

Nobody wants to lose. "Winning is the name of the game"—that's what they say in sports. Who wants to run a race and come in last?

If it is worth the effort to become a Christian in the first place it is worth living that life one hundred percent. And it *can* be. God doesn't want any of His children to be losers, and they don't have to be. By His grace we can "go over," not under.

It is not unusual to hear someone say, "I'd like to be saved, but I'm afraid I couldn't live it." A person is to be admired for not wanting to start the spiritual race and not finish. Maybe we can say a few things in this chapter to let you know that victory, and nothing but victory, is God's plan for every Christian.

Don't look wistfully at someone who is a strong Christian and say, "I wish I could be like that, but I know I can't." We don't live victoriously by comparing ourselves with others. God doesn't ask us to set impossible goals. Failure isn't in His blueprint for us. But we have to follow His way, not ours.

If you are one who has tried the Christian life and think you have failed, don't think this puts you on the Lord's blacklist. We don't win by crying over spilt milk. Let's see what God says about winning, and then get with it!

## CHRIST DID IT

Spiritual victory is based on the believer's identification with Christ. It is because He is victor that His followers can be too. It is futile to try to struggle to the top through our own efforts. We don't have to fight for a victory that has already been won by our Saviour!

It is vital that we steer clear of self-reliance. "Not I, but Christ," Paul declared in Galatians 2:20.

Here's some good Scripture to start with: "So you have everything when you have Christ, and you are filled with God through your union with Christ. He is the highest Ruler, with authority over every other power. When you came to Christ he set you free from your evil desires, not by a bodily operation of circumcision but by a spiritual operation, the baptism of your souls. For in baptism you see how your old evil nature died with him and was buried with him; and then you came up out of death with him into a new life because you trusted the Word of the mighty God who raised Christ from the dead" (Colossians 2:10-12, *Living Bible Paraphrased*).

That bears repeating: "You have everything when you have Christ!" Belonging to Jesus is like having the master key that unlocks every door in the building. He came to this world because there was no one else who could reconcile God and man. No human could save another human because each one is a sinner. It took someone sinless to pay the price of redemption, and Jesus was that One. Now that the price has been paid we only need to come to Him to have the doors of every spiritual treasure-house opened to us.

Jesus taught us to pray in His name. This operates on the same principle as a rich man signing his name at the bottom of a blank check and letting you fill in your name and the amount. We are spiritual paupers, but Christ is heir of His Father's riches. When we accept Him we share in those riches. Sound too good to be true? Probably so, but it *is* true. The gospel is no small thing!

When Jesus cried "It is finished" on the cross He meant just that. The plan of redemption was completed. The full price was paid. We don't have to add a thing. In fact, anything we add would be worthless.

This is why the New Testament says so much about grace. If we could do something ourselves that would save us and give us victory, no grace would be involved. It would be our doing; our ability; our cleverness. But since we are unable to earn salvation or be overcomers in our own strength, it all has to come from God. This is grace. Sometimes we call it "unmerited favor."

## SATAN IN RETREAT

"You were dead in sins, and your sinful desires were not yet cut away. Then he gave you a share in the very life of Christ, for he forgave all your sins, and blotted out the charges proved against you, the list of his commandments which you had not obeyed. He took this list of sins and destroyed it by nailing it to Christ's cross. In this way God took away Satan's power to accuse you of sin, and God openly displayed to the whole world Christ's triumph at the cross where your sins were all taken away" (Colossians 2:13-15, *Living Bible Paraphrased*).

Christ's victory over Satan was necessary because Satan had rebelled against God. Originally Satan was the "anointed cherub" (Ezekiel 28:14). Tragically he decided to try to take God's throne from Him (Isaiah 14:13). This resulted in his fall, but he has never given up trying to defeat God. When Jesus died and rose again He dealt Satan the blow that means his final defeat. The Resurrection was also necessary to assure victory over Satan. We share in the triumph of a resurrected Lord.

Of course the ultimate judgment has not fallen on Satan yet, so he still wages war against God's people. It is a losing war, as the above passage of Scripture tells us. Our part is to claim the victory that Jesus has already won for us over the devil.

The first prophecy concerning Christ is in Genesis 3:15. It is thrilling to note that God was talking to Satan when He spoke these words: "And I will put enmity between thee and the woman, and between thy seed and her seed; it shall bruise thy head, and thou shalt bruise his heel."

A person does not die from a bruised heel. Jesus was bruised and even put to death on the cross. But death could not hold Him. When God said the Messiah would bruise Satan's head He meant literally *"crush thy head."* A crushed head means death. Satan cannot forget those words, and is constantly trying to overthrow God's work in spite of them. We cannot fight him in our own power, but he cannot stand against Christ. This means that we must constantly remind ourselves that Jesus stands between us and the devil.

Christ came to bring freedom. It is not His desire that people remain in slavery to Satan. Nor does He wish for His children to be defeated by this enemy at any time. Jesus was talking about His mission of crushing Satan when He said, "Now is the judgment of this world; now shall the prince of this world be cast out" (John 12:31).

## DON'T TRY IT ALONE

Maybe it sounds as though we're repeating, and we are. It is so hard for us to realize that our victory is so wrapped up in Christ's victory that we *need* to have it repeated.

Many who believe in Christ do not realize how complete the victory is which they have in Him. They try to live victoriously by their own efforts. In their attempt to achieve success they establish rules. Paul points out the inconsistency of trying to gain victory in this manner in this passage:

"Since you died, as it were, with Christ and this has set you free from following the world's ideas of how to be saved—by doing good and obeying various rules—why do you keep right on following them anyway, still bound by such rules as not eating, tasting, or even touching certain foods? Such rules are mere human teachings, for food was made to be eaten and used up. These rules may seem good, for rules of this kind require strong devotion and are humiliating and hard on the body, but they have no effect when it comes to conquering a person's evil thoughts and desires. They only make him proud" (Colossians 2: 20-23, *Living Bible Paraphrased*).

See the difference? Here is a Christian continually making rules and trying to keep them. It makes him feel holy. Unfortunately he is not able to keep all of them, and every time he breaks one he is discouraged. He decides, "There's no use. I give up." If he does not follow this route, he pretends he *is* keeping all the rules and becomes as self-righteous as a Pharisee.

But here is another Christian who relaxes in the knowledge that Christ has kept all of God's rules and that as long as he stays close to Him he will receive His power to overcome. If he makes a mistake he asks forgiveness and knows that Jesus' blood will cleanse him. It is not rule keeping, but living close to Christ, that enables him to stay on top.

"Since you became alive again, so to speak, when Christ arose from the dead, now set your sights on the rich treasures and joys of heaven where he sits beside God in the place of honor and power. Let heaven fill your thoughts; don't spend your time worrying about things down here. You should have as little desire for this world as a dead person does. Your real life is in heaven with Christ and God" (Colossians 3:1-3, *Living Bible Paraphrased*).

## A STEP AT A TIME

When we accept Christ a new life begins. In many ways it is like a new physical life. We must learn to walk spiritually, just as we learn to walk with our feet. The first step may be a little shaky. But the second one is easier, and finally a child learns to walk with confidence.

As Christians we do well to remember that we take one step at a time. The God who gives us strength for the first step will give strength for all the steps that follow.

There may be some things over which we get the victory more easily than others. But we should not be satisfied until all of the things God calls "sin" are eliminated from our lives. Sexual impurity, uncleanness, passion, evil desires, covetousness, anger, wrath, malice, blasphemy or abusive language, foul talk, and lying, are among those sins that must not be present in the life of the one who would serve the Lord Jesus.

A Christian realizes that he is not only dead with Christ but also alive with Christ. Consequently he displays the qualities of a new life. He is merciful, kind, humble, meek, long-suffering, forbearing, loving, and peaceful. He has "put on" these qualities (Colossians 3:12-15).

A life of consistent prayer and Bible study is a "must" if we are to be victorious Christians. This takes self-discipline, but it is worth it. We do not reach spiritual goals by wishful thinking.

If the Lord is to do everything for us that He desires, it is obvious that we must be completely yielded to Him. We must not argue with His will. When we find instructions in the Bible we must determine to live by them instead of trying to find a way around them.

We must not be discouraged by seeming failures, nor become overconfident when we enjoy success. As surely as we become puffed up over a victory the Lord will let us stub our toe a time or two. This is to let us know that it is still His power, not ours, that gets the job done!

Every step we take in the Christian life is a step of faith. God doesn't show us the road for a mile ahead. Each day is a new step. By faith we take the step, knowing that the Lord will be with us. Each day brings new battles, but it also brings new grace.

### But Isn't This Asking Too Much?

"This is a new day. Times are different. We have to change with the world."

Ever hear those words? Some people use them as an excuse for living a Christian life that is sloppy and halfhearted. They complain that it just isn't practical to talk about spiritual victory in days like ours.

Are the words of the Bible only for people of ancient times? Must we float with the current and submit meekly to public opinion because we live in the 20th century instead of the first?

A thousand times no! Every age has had its problems and special temptations. We just happen to be a little more advanced scientifically. We've been to the moon you know! All of this doesn't change our basic needs, nor does it alter God's power.

Sin is sin in any century. God will not tolerate undisciplined living now any more than He did in Paul's day.

There is a lot of satisfaction in bucking the tide. And make no mistake about it, people still admire a man or woman with convictions. There's a good feeling about being the only one in the crowd who desn't light up a cigarette or down a glass of beer. There's real satisfaction in being the one who doesn't tell the dirty joke nor smile at it.

Some day the person you think has the hardest heart may beat a path to your door and ask you to pray for him—providing you have lived a consistent life in front of him. Often the one who sneered a little will see the hour when he will want your spiritual support. Not everyone is as tough as he pretends. That skeptic may be hoping with all of his heart that you stand true!

It's no disgrace to be different. The Christian *will* be different. God demands it. Why be poured into the same mold as everyone around you? Why be a parrot? Why look and act like every Tom, Dick, and Harry in the crowd?

We aren't talking about mere church-joining. We're talking about *new life!*

If you're going to be a Christian at all, be the best one you can be with God's help. The world today is cursed with mediocrity. Don't be a mediocre Christian. Be one that will delight your Heavenly Father.

Haven't you noticed a monotonous sameness about people who are part of the devil's crowd? Many of them seem like robots. But they'll sit up and take notice when they see a real, live, sure-enough Christian who isn't ashamed of what the Lord has done for him!

## Look What's Ahead!

"When Christ, who is our life, shall apear, then shall ye also appear with him in glory" (Colossians 3:4).

What a future we have as Christians! This present life with Christ is wonderful, but it isn't the end. The best is yet to come when we're through with earth.

The crowning reward of our Christian life will be seeing Jesus. Often we speculate about heaven. Some talk of the crown they hope to wear or the mansion where they will live. Actually the greatest thing about heaven will be the presence of our Lord.

This verse says we shall appear with Christ in glory. It is impossible for us to know all that this involves. It is beyond our comprehension. The word "glory" is too big for human imagination. It will not be for a moment and then gone, like a bubble that has burst. It will be forever.

We have mentioned being united with Christ in His death and resurrection. This same union continues through eternity. We shall be with Him in glory.

A goal like this makes it easier to take the hard knocks of life. The trials lose some of their sting when we think about what is coming. Compared with eternity, this life is just a little while. The tests are coming to an end. The hard work will be over some day. Then we will be glad we did not give up when we were only part of the way home.

"Christ, who is our life!" He is the center of our whole experience. He is the Author and Finisher of our faith. He began the work of salvation in us, and He will bring it to a victorious conclusion.

Does it really matter, then, if we have to give up a few things for His sake? Is it really so bad if we even undergo some persecution for our faith? The "glory" that is waiting will make us forget all of these things in a hurry.

# 5
# Let's Go
# to the Upper Room

Where does a Christian's power come from? From his own brains or brawn? Anyone will shout "No" to that one!

Our power comes from one source, and *only* one —the Holy Spirit. He doesn't give natural power. What He produces is supernatural. This is what we must have to influence men toward God by our testimony. It's what we have to possess to overcome the sin around us.

In Old Testament days the Holy Spirit came upon men from time to time, but then seemed to withdraw. He did not stay in their lives as a permanent resident. We might say He came and went as far as individuals were concerned.

But God promised a new age in which the Holy Spirit would come to live permanently in the lives of men who turned to Jesus as Saviour. In fact He went so far as to say that the Holy Spirit would make redeemed men His temples (1 Corinthians 3:16,17).

This new age started with the Day of Pentecost recorded in the second chapter of Acts. This is what we'll be talking about in this chapter. It happened in what was called "an upper room" (Acts 1:13).

And it has been happening ever since! Has it happened to you?

## JOEL SAW IT COMING

Here is the great Pentecostal prophecy of the Old Testament. Peter quoted it on the Day of Pentecost. All Christians need to read it often:

"And it shall come to pass afterward, that I will pour out my Spirit upon all flesh; and your sons and your daughters shall prophesy, your old men shall dream dreams, your young men shall see visions: and also upon the servants and upon the handmaids in those days will I pour out my Spirit.

"And I will show wonders in the heavens and in the earth, blood, and fire, and pillars of smoke. The sun shall be turned into darkness, and the moon into blood, before the great and the terrible day of the Lord come. And it shall come to pass, that whosoever shall call upon the name of the Lord shall be delivered: for in mount Zion and in Jerusalem shall be deliverance, as the Lord hath said, and in the remnant whom the Lord shall call" (Joel 2:28-32).

It was Joel's pen that wrote these words, but it was God who moved upon him to do it. This prophecy was given several hundred years before the outpouring of the Spirit recorded in Acts.

The centuries that elapsed between the giving of this promise and its fulfillment were not wasted. God used them to prepare the way for the fulfillment of the prophecy. Before He sent forth His Holy Spirit it was His plan to send His Son. Before He sent His Son He prepared the way for Him. Paul said, "But when the fulness of the time was come, God sent forth His Son" (Galatians 4:4). When Jesus came the time for the outpouring of the Holy Spirit was not far away.

46

Why must Jesus come before the Holy Spirit could be poured out upon all flesh? Because the Spirit can only come on prepared people. There must be repentance and a turning from sin. There must be the cleansing of that sin. Only Jesus can do this. His blood was shed for this purpose. He said He came to build a church (Matthew 16:18). The Holy Spirit brought that church into being on the Day of Pentecost.

Joel's promise was that the Spirit would be poured out "upon all flesh." This means that the Spirit is available to everyone, with no exceptions. The fact that all do not accept is not God's fault, but theirs. There is no class nor age distinction. It is for sons and daughters, young men and old men, servants and handmaidens. You can put yourself right in the middle of the picture!

### Jesus Said, "He's Almost Here."

When someone knows he is going to die soon, he will talk about the things nearest to his heart. One of the subjects Jesus talked about most just before His death was the coming of the Holy Spirit. There are three consecutive chapters in John's Gospel (14, 15, and 16) where our Lord speaks of the Spirit's coming again and again.

The disciples were very disturbed because Jesus was going to leave them. But He said, "I will pray the Father and he shall give you another Comforter, that he may abide with you for ever; even the Spirit of truth; whom the world cannot receive, because it seeth him not, neither knoweth him: but ye know him; for he dwelleth with you, and shall be in you. I will not leave you comfortless: I will come to you" (John 16:16-18).

Later that evening Jesus said more to His dis-

47

ciples about the Holy Spirit: "Nevertheless I tell you the truth; It is expedient for you that I go away: for if I go not away, the Comforter will not come unto you; but if I depart, I will send him unto you" (John 16:7).

After His resurrection, and before His ascension, Jesus again promised the coming of the Holy Spirit. It is worth noting that He called the outpouring of the Spirit "the promise of my Father" (Luke 24:49). The Father has made many promises, but Jesus singled out the coming of the Spirit as *the* promise. Undoubtedly this is because it is one of the greatest promises in the Bible.

Shortly before He went up through the clouds and back to heaven Jesus spoke on the subject again: "But ye shall receive power, after that the Holy Ghost is come upon you: and ye shall be witnesses unto me both in Jerusalem, and in all Judea, and in Samaria, and unto the uttermost part of the earth" (Acts 1:8).

In His references to the coming of the Spirit Jesus indicated that some conditions had to be fulfilled first:

1. A people had to be ready. This was because the Holy Spirit is one "whom the world cannot receive, because it seeth him not, neither knoweth him" (John 14:17). As the life of Jesus on earth drew to its close a people had been made ready for the coming of the Holy Spirit. The believers were looking for Him. The Holy Spirit comes to indwell people at salvation. The baptism in the Spirit comes to those already saved and cleansed.

2. Jesus had to ascend to the Father. Peter declared at Pentecost: "This Jesus hath God raised up. . . . Therefore being by the right hand of God ex-

alted, and having received of the Father the promise of the Holy Ghost, he hath shed forth this, which ye now see and hear" (Acts 2:32,33).

3. The disciples had to wait at Jerusalem. "Behold, I send the promise of my Father upon you: but tarry ye in the city of Jerusalem, until ye be endued with power from on high" (Luke 24:49).

The disciples waited, or tarried, about 10 days at Jerusalem before the Holy Spirit descended upon them at Pentecost. (Pentecost was 50 days after Passover. Jesus was crucified on the Day of the Passover and was seen by the disciples for about 40 days before His ascension (Acts 1:3). Fifty days minus 40 leaves 10 days as the period of tarrying, or waiting, at Jerusalem for the coming of the Holy Spirit.)

## A CITY CRIED: "WHAT HIT US?"

"And when the day of Pentecost was fully come, they were all with one accord in one place. And suddenly there came a sound from heaven as of a rushing mighty wind, and it filled all the house where they were sitting. And there appeared unto them cloven tongues like as of fire, and it sat upon each of them. And they were all filled with the Holy Ghost, and began to speak with other tongues, as the Spirit gave them utterance" (Acts 2:1-4).

It didn't take long for the news to spread. When it did, thousands of people began milling around the Upper Room. By this time the disciples were outside. Every one of them was so full of the Spirit that all he could do was praise the Lord. The startling thing was that he was not doing it in his own language. The onlookers asked, "And how hear we every man in our own tongue, wherein we were born?" (Acts 2:8).

People had swarmed into Jerusalem by the thousand from various parts of the world for the religious feasts. They came from countries that spoke different languages. Now they were hearing these Jewish believers tell of God's wonderful works in the languages of the countries where they lived (Acts 2:9-11).

The disciples had not gone to school and learned those languages. The Holy Spirit was speaking through them supernaturally. They did not know what they were saying, but the Spirit did.

How would *your* city react to something like this? Probably about the same way the people of Jerusalem did. You can almost hear them gasp as they cried, "What meaneth this?" (Acts 2:12).

Naturally there was some wisecracking about the Christians simply being drunk (Acts 2:13), but it is doubtful whether many believed this. It was too awesome for such a simple explanation.

THE FIRST EVIDENCE

What was the first sign that the Holy Spirit had come? It was the speaking in other tongues. This was not the last time this phenomenon occurred. In fact every time an outward sign is mentioned in the Book of Acts it is speaking in tongues. This is why Pentecostal churches believe and teach that the initial physical evidence of the baptism in the Holy Spirit is speaking in other tongues.

Turn to the tenth chapter of Acts. The whole chapter is the thrilling story of God's response to a Gentile named Cornelius, who sought Him with all his heart. Because of the devotion of this man, who was a Roman army officer, God sent Peter to his house to explain the gospel. Here's what happened:

"While Peter yet spake these words, the Holy Ghost

fell on all them which heard the word. And they of the circumcision which believed were astonished, as many as came with Peter, because that on the Gentiles also was poured out the gift of the Holy Ghost. For they heard them speak with tongues, and magnify God" (Acts 10:44-46).

There you have it: Speaking in tongues again. This was how a strict Jew like Peter knew that Gentiles had been accepted by the Lord. It convinced him so completely of their salvation that he immediately ordered them baptized (Acts 10:47,48).

You should also read Acts 19:1-7. It's an eye-opening story of a dozen men at Ephesus who seemed to be believers but were obviously lacking something. When Paul questioned them, "Have ye received the Holy Ghost since ye believed?" they answered, "We have not so much as heard whether there be any Holy Ghost."

These were disciples of John the Baptist, who did not understand what Jesus had done. When Paul explained the gospel and laid hands on them they were filled with the Spirit. What was the first outward evidence? "They spake with tongues, and prophesied" (Acts 19:6).

There are two other accounts in Acts of Christians being filled with the Spirit—in chapters 8 and 9. These passages do not specifically mention any outward sign. Some argue that this means tongues is not necessarily the evidence. Such reasoning is not sound. When I tell someone about an individual who was filled with the Spirit I do not always add the information that he spoke in tongues. This is understood, and does not need to be repeated every time.

If you will read Acts 8:18,19 you will notice that some unusual sign *did* occur when those Samaritans were filled with the Spirit. It was so amazing that a religious racketeer named Simon was willing to pay money for the power to make it happen when he wanted it to. Was the sign speaking in tongues? Pentecostals believe so. What else could it have been that was so startling to a sorcerer?

In Acts 9 it is an individual—Saul of Tarsus, later to be named Paul—who was filled with the Spirit (v. 17). No sign is mentioned. But years later Paul declared to the Corinthians, "I speak with tongues more than ye all" (1 Corinthians 14:18). When did he start? Pentecostals have no doubt that it was at that moment when he was first filled.

## THE ULTIMATE EVIDENCE

While speaking in tongues is the first outward sign of the Spirit's infilling, we must not be content for it to be the *only* evidence.

The ultimate evidence is power (Acts 1:8). Jesus said this power will make us witnesses for Him. The baptism in the Holy Spirit will give force to our testimony. Not every one to whom we testify will be saved, but many will be.

Peter denied his Lord three times before His crucifixion. Yet on the Day of Pentecost the same man stood before 3,000 people and proclaimed Jesus as the risen Saviour. What made the change? Power! Where did it come from? The Holy Spirit was now in full possession of Peter.

The power that brought 3,000 into the church at Pentecost was not exhausted then. After this it is recorded that "the Lord added to the church daily such as should be saved" (Acts 2:47).

The baptism in the Holy Spirit gave those early Christians power in prayer. In Acts 4:31 we read that "when they had prayed, the place was shaken where they were assembled together; and they were all filled with the Holy Ghost, and they spake the word of God with boldness."

There was no end to it. We read in Acts 4:33, "And with great power gave the apostles witness of the resurrection of the Lord Jesus: and great grace was upon them all." It all started at Pentecost. But it was *only* the start. It was like a river that kept getting broader and deeper the farther it flowed.

The baptism in the Holy Spirit gives power for overcoming spiritual and moral opposition. There is no greater example than the first Christian martyr, Stephen. How could a man pray for his executioners and go out of this world with his eyes on heaven? (Acts 7:56-60). This was the story of Stephen, and there was only one answer: He was full of the Holy Ghost (Acts 7:55).

## WHO'S IT FOR?

"This is all great, but what does it have to do with me? The age of the apostles is over."

Ever hear someone put up this kind of excuse? How unfortunate for a Christian to deprive himself of his spiritual birthright. What belonged to the Early Church is ours, too. There is not an iota of scriptural support for the argument that the baptism in the Holy Spirit was only for those of the first century.

How could the Lord put it any plainer than when He used Peter to fling out this banner: "Repent, and be baptized every one of you in the name of Jesus Christ for the remission of sins, and ye shall receive the gift of the Holy Ghost. For the promise is unto you, and to your children, and to all that are afar off, even as many as the Lord our God shall call" (Acts 2:38,39).

It just isn't possible to be any plainer. God has

provided the baptism in the Holy Spirit for every believer. He continues to baptize Christians in the Holy Spirit because He still needs witnesses with power.

God has no specific waiting period before a person can be filled with the Spirit. He is ready to baptize the Christian in the Spirit as soon as that person is ready. At Caesarea those hearing Peter preach were baptized in the Spirit as soon as they believed. In fact it happened while Peter was still preaching (Acts 10:34-47). In other instances a delay was involved. The crucial issue is not the amount of time that must be spent in waiting, but the degree of individual spiritual readiness.

"Tarrying" or "waiting" for the baptism in the Holy Spirit is not to get God ready, but to get *you* ready. Your "Upper Room" can be any place you want to make it. How about right where you are now?

# 6
# For the Good of All

"Now concerning spiritual gifts, brethren, I would not have you ignorant" (1 Corinthians 12:1). Plain enough, isn't it? God doesn't want any misunderstanding about spiritual gifts. There was plenty of confusion in the Corinthian church about the gifts, and it was causing nothing but chaos.

There's no question that the gifts of the Spirit should be present in the church today. Just because we live nearly 2,000 years later than the Corinthian Christians doesn't mean we can't get mixed up along these lines, too. A lot of us do. Why did Paul say he did not want us ignorant about spiritual gifts? Because such ignorance invites confusion and fanaticism.

Here is a principle we must never forget: "Now there are diversities of gifts, but the same Spirit" (1 Corinthians 12:4). In your home you may have an electric stove, a refrigerator, lights, and an air conditioner. Each one has a different purpose. But all get their power from the same source. Each appliance represents a different manifestation of electricity.

The gifts of the Spirit may be different, but one

Holy Spirit is the source of them all. They are different expressions of His power and presence.

"There are differences of administrations, but the same Lord" (1 Corinthians 12:5). This means there are different kinds of service to God, but the same Lord provides the ability to perform the varied services. No one should envy another because his ability, or gift, is different.

There is no better illustration than the human body. Paul makes this very point: "For as the body is one, and hath many members and all the members of that one body, being many, are one body: so also is Christ" (1 Corinthians 12:12).

The foot, the hand, the head, the eye, the ear—all have different functions. But all are a part of one body.

If we were one big ear, we couldn't see. If we were all foot we couldn't reach out to grasp anything. God has put the body together so that each part, large or small, has a job to do. Paul says the church is like the human body. No one should worry whether he is a hand, a foot or an eye as long as he is doing the job God gave him.

## LET'S FILL OUR PLACE

Notice 1 Corinthians 12:6: "And there are diversities of operations, but it is the same God which worketh all in all." The *Living Bible Paraphrased* puts it this way: "There are many ways in which God works in our lives, but it is the same God who does the work in and through all of us who are his." That's the same thing Paul says later in his discussion about the human body and its parts.

"But the manifestation of the Spirit is given to every man to profit withal" (1 Corinthians 12:7). This means that God bestows spiritual gifts upon individuals for a purpose. That purpose is *the common good of the church;* the profit of every member. We'll talk more about this later.

If we know the purpose of the gifts it will help us to use them correctly. Each gift is a ministry. A ministry is a means of service. And "service" is what the Christian life is all about.

## It's His Decision

After Paul lists the gifts of the Spirit, he writes, "But all these worketh that one and the selfsame Spirit, dividing to every man severally as he will" (1 Corinthians 12:11). This means that the Holy Spirit knows best what gift each Christian should have. They are *His* gifts; not ours. Paul names nine distinct spiritual gifts, each of them contributing to the welfare of the church.

Since the apostle does not explain each gift, it would seem that the best way to find examples is in the Book of Acts. It is reasonable to assume that we will see instances in Acts where the gifts are manifested. Naturally the Scripture does not say, "This is an example of the word of wisdom, etc." We must rely on the Spirit's guidance as we compare Scripture with Scripture and dig out the truth for ourselves.

### THE WORD OF WISDOM

This does not mean that God simply makes us wiser. We are talking about a supernaturally inspired utterance of wisdom. An example is found in the 15th chapter of Acts. The church had reached a virtual stalemate in its deliberations about Christians keeping the Law of Moses. Then it happened. The apostle James began to speak. When he finished, the matter was settled. The Holy Spirit had given him the word of wisdom. It was not something James had studied and worked out for himself. It was the Spirit using his mind and lips. Read the whole passage (Acts 15: 13-22) and you will be thrilled to see how the Holy Spirit solved the dilemma.

THE WORD OF KNOWLEDGE

There are times when spiritual information is needed. The Holy Spirit at such times gives the word of knowledge to a member of the church. Through this gift there are revealed certain facts of God's all-embracing knowledge that could not otherwise be known. It may be difficult to determine the difference between knowledge and wisdom for they are closely related.

When Peter, on the Day of Pentecost, quoted Joel's prophecy and explained that it was then being fulfilled, this was probably the word of knowledge (Acts 2:16-21). Since the Word of God is the basis of all knowledge, it would seem that this spiritual gift would relate to knowledge in the Word.

FAITH

This does not refer to saving faith in general, for God gives this to all Christians. The faith here is what we would call wonder-working faith. This is faith directed toward some special end. It may often be linked with healing, but not always.

Peter undoubtedly was being used in the exercise of miraculous faith when he took the lame man by the hand and lifted him up (Acts 3:1-11). This faith had to come before the healing took place.

GIFTS OF HEALING

Notice that this is plural. It is not "the gift" of healing, but "gifts." This would seem to imply that provision has been made for the healing of different kinds of sicknesses. Gifts of healing are God's provision for believers' physical well-being. They are to be used "to profit withal," or "for the common good," of the body of Christ (1 Corinthians 12:7,12,27).

## THE WORKING OF MIRACLES

Miracles are "deeds of power." They are other than healings, for healings have already been mentioned in the list. Possibly the casting out of demons would be included in this gift.

## PROPHECY

In the Old Testament, prophecy was often the foretelling of the future. In the New Testament it usually means "forthtelling." It is the utterance of inspired exhortations, instructions, and warnings. The primary purpose of prophecy is to edify (build up), to exhort (encourage), and to comfort (console) (1 Corinthians 14:3).

Prophecy is distinct from revelation, from knowledge, and from doctrine, or teaching (1 Corinthians 14:6). Although it may have an effect on the unbeliever (1 Corinthians 14:24,25) prophecy is primarily for the church and its members (1 Corinthians 14: 4,22).

Again, we must remember that we are talking about a supernatural gift. Prophecy is not simply telling something we have thought of. It is more than a testimony. It is usually a sudden, forceful utterance. It does not consist of words that are premeditated, but given at the moment by the Spirit.

## DISCERNING OF SPIRITS

It should be noted that this is not referred to in

the Bible as "the gift of discernment." It is "discerning of spirits." There is a great difference.

Through this gift it is brought to light whether the Holy Spirit or false spirits, or the human spirit, are behind the actions and words of certain individuals.

There is no better example than what is recorded in Acts 16:16-18. A young lady was following Paul and his companions and crying that they were the servants of the Most High God. What she was saying was true, but it was given in a spirit of harassment. Paul discerned that she was being influenced by an evil spirit, not the Spirit of God.

In other words, this gift enables a Christian, by the supernatural power of the Spirit, to tell the difference between the real and the counterfeit in the spiritual realm.

### DIVERS KINDS OF TONGUES

Paul is not here discussing tongues as the initial physical evidence of the baptism in the Holy Spirit. The subject is the exercise of the *gift* of tongues in a church where people have already been filled with the Spirit. The gift of speaking in tongues is sometimes confused with speaking in tongues as the first outward sign of the Spirit's infilling. The two are the same in essence, but different in purpose and use. It is not correct to refer to the baptism in the Holy Spirit as the receiving of "the gift of tongues."

### THE INTERPRETATION OF TONGUES

This gift is a supplement to the gift of tongues. It enables people to understand what has been said in tongues. If there is no interpretation the church cannot profit from the utterance in tongues.

"Brethren, be not children in understanding: howbeit in malice be ye children, but in understanding be men" (1 Corinthians 14:20).

When it comes to planning evil, we are to be as innocent as children. But in our understanding of spiritual truths we are to be grown-up. Children love toys, and spiritual gifts are not toys for immature believers to play with.

God has established several general principles to cover the use of the gifts. For one thing, they are to be used intelligently. "I would not have you ignorant," the Word says. "In understanding be men." God does not take away our minds, nor erase our common sense. He is intelligent, and expects us to be intelligent in the exercise of spiritual gifts.

The gifts should be used lovingly. The "more excellent way" (1 Corinthians 12:31) is the way of charity, or love. The gifts must not be used maliciously. There should be no rivalry in their exercise. This promotes divisions and confusion. Spiritual gifts are not for the purpose of enabling Christians to "show off."

The gifts should be used for the good of all. This is the great basic principle. Selfishness has no place in the use of the gifts. They should be used for the good of everyone, or they should not be used at all in public (1 Corinthians 14:27,28).

The gifts should be used for edification. "Let all things be done unto edifying" (1 Corinthians 14:26). The gifts may be used privately for personal edification, but when used publicly they should edify, or build up, all of the church. This is what Paul meant when he said, "Seek that ye may excel to the edifying of the church" (1 Corinthians 14:12).

Some of the gifts were being misused at Corinth, especially tongues and prophecy. Tongues was probably the most misused of all. Otherwise Paul would not have given so much space to corrective teaching about tongues.

For one thing there was speaking in tongues without interpretation. The person speaking in tongues was helped because he was speaking in the Spirit to God. However, the church was not being helped because there was no understanding of what was being said (1 Corinthians 14:2-11,15,16).

To correct the condition, Paul instructed, "Wherefore, let him that speaketh in an unknown tongue pray that he may interpret" (1 Corinthians 14:13, compare 14:5,9,15,16). Here is further instruction: "But if there be no interpreter, let him keep silence in the church, and let him speak to himself and to God" (1 Corinthians 14:28).

All were speaking in tongues at the same time in the services at Corinth. "If therefore the whole assembly comes together at one time and all should be speaking in tongues, and uninstructed ones, or unbelievers, should come in, will they not say that you are mad?" (1 Corinthians 14:23, literal translation). To correct the condition, Paul instructed, "If any man speak in an unknown tongue, let it be by two, or at the most by three, and that by course; and let one interpret" (1 Corinthians 14:27).

CARRYING A GOOD THING TO AN EXTREME

There was an excess of speaking in tongues at Corinth. Consequently, Paul instructed that the number of utterances be limited to two or three—as you will note in the above Scripture verse.

The gift of prophecy was also being misused. Ev-

everyone was prophesying at the same time. Paul commanded, "Let the prophets speak two or three, and let the other judge. If anything be revealed to another that sitteth by, let the first hold his peace" (1 Corinthians 14:29,30). Actually, this was simply telling the people to use good manners! The Holy Spirit does not cause anyone to behave in an offensive way.

In case anyone said, "I can't control myself," Paul's word was, "And the spirits of the prophets are subject to the prophets." He was saying, "You can, and you must, control yourselves."

Finally, the apostle laid down a rule that is as valid today as then: "Let all things be done decently and in order" (1 Corinthians 14:40).

## STRIVING FOR EXCELLENCE

"But covet earnestly the best gifts. And yet show I unto you a more excellent way" (1 Corinthians 12:31).

The gifts of the Spirit are extremely important to the spiritual life of the church. Paul did not call for elimination of the gifts but for their regulation. Paul says, "Covet earnestly," or "Be eager to possess," the best gifts. All gifts are valuable, but they are not of *equal* value. For example, speaking in tongues plus the interpretation of tongues, taken together, are loosely equal to the one gift of prophecy (1 Corinthians 14:5). Here is the point to remember: *the value of a gift depends upon the degree to which it is able to build up the church.* Paul wanted these gifts to be used, but used in the right way. He insisted that they be used intelligently, lovingly, in an orderly manner, for edification, and for the good of all. Remember: these are the gifts of the *Spirit*. They are too valuable to be misused.

It is no accident that the great love chapter—1 Corinthians 13—is sandwiched in between chapters 12 and 14, which deal in detail with spiritual gifts. What the apostle is saying is "You want the gifts. That's fine. Go on desiring them. But a better way is to desire to use them for the good of all."

# 7

# When You're Sick, He cares

If we had our way there would be no sickness, would there? Small illnesses are annoying; big ones can be disastrous. But, like it or not, sickness is a fact of life. If we haven't faced it the chances are we will.

Usually we use the term "divine healing" when we're talking about praying for the sick. If anyone wants to prove that God doesn't heal today he won't find that proof in the Bible. If God redeems a man's soul is it outlandish to think He can heal his body?

Never forget that the Lord is interested in the whole man. If you are a whole man you are a body as well as a spirit and a mind. Who can imagine a merciful God being unconcerned about any part of us?

One Scripture verse often quoted when folks talk about divine healing is Hebrews 13:8: "Jesus Christ the same yesterday, and today, and for ever." That's a good one. Jesus healed the sick when He was here on earth. That was a good many "yesterdays" ago, but a thousand years are as a day to the Lord. He doesn't reckon time as we do. Twenty centuries do not alter the power nor the compassion of our Saviour.

The Early Church had a great healing ministry. It covers the whole Book of Acts, so we won't try to quote the whole account. Before He ascended, Jesus promised to His disciples that they would lay hands on the sick and see them recover (Mark 16:18). Such signs, Jesus said, will follow "them that believe" (Mark 16:17). So the promise wasn't just to the apostles. If you believe on Jesus Christ as your personal Saviour you are included.

Don't live below your privileges as a Christian. If God has promised you something, claim it in the name of Jesus. It would be a pity to let Satan give you an inferiority complex. You're God's child as much as Peter, James, John, and all of the first century believers. Aren't you?

Let's never regard divine healing as a strange, mystical something to be used only by a few who belong to some kind of inner circle. It's a privilege to be claimed by believers in everyday life when the need arises. We need not wait until some catastrophic illness strikes. Why not believe God for every physical ailment, large or small?

## How Did It Start?

Obviously God did not want sickness in the world. His creation was perfect. There was no sickness nor death. There wasn't even any pain. In fact the soil didn't sprout weeds or thorns. It was a beautiful picture.

But something spoiled the perfection. That "something" has three letters, but it's the deadliest word in our language—*sin*. And sin has an author—just as a book has one. It's Satan. That's another terrible name, but one we have to reckon with.

When man obeyed Satan instead of God he had a fall. It affected him spiritually first of all. It made

66

him susceptible to the suggestions of the devil. Every man since Adam has been born with the seeds of sin planted in his being. When he comes to the age of accountability the seed sprouts and grows. He becomes a sinner.

The Fall affected man physically, also. If he had not sinned he would never have died. But all that changed. It isn't long after the account of the Fall that you begin to read in the Book of Genesis about people dying. At first the human life span was nearly a thousand years. Gradually it got shorter and shorter. Every kind of misery and trouble in our world today stems from that one tragic event in the Garden of Eden. When Adam and Eve said yes to Satan the world was plunged into a horrible mess.

God had warned the first humans not to eat the fruit of the tree of knowledge of good and evil. "In the day that thou eatest thereof thou shalt surely die," He reminded them (Genesis 2:17). The death penalty included physical death as well as spiritual death.

Sickness came automatically when death walked in the door. "Dust thou art, and unto dust shalt thou return," God told Adam (Genesis 3:19). Sickness is simply a reminder of the death that is sure to come some day.

Sickness will remain a peril to man until the time when "this corruptible shall have put on incorruption, and this mortal shall have put on immortality." When that happens, "then shall be brought to pass the saying that is written, Death is swallowed up in victory." Even now, believers can sing, "O death, where is thy sting? O grave, where is thy victory?" (1 Corinthians 15:55). But until the curse for sin is finally removed, men will get sick. And they will die. God never wanted it this way. In the gospel He has made provisions for dealing with both sickness and death.

## WHY DOES IT HAPPEN?

There is a certain mystery about sickness. It does little good to spend all of our time speculating about "why?" But it may help us to think of a few basic reasons why people get sick:

1. For one thing, there is an inherent weakness in our bodies that makes us susceptible to illness. How fortunate we are if our physical constitution has held up well. But the weakness is there, and may appear at any time. It is a part of being human. It is because sin's curse is still with us.

2. For the Christian, God may use sickness to work out something that could not be dealt with in any other way. If Romans 8:28 is true, then some good has to come from sickness as well as other unpleasant things. Do you remember that promise? "And we know that all things work together for good to them that love God, to them who are the called according to his purpose." If you get sick, don't forget that verse!

3. Sickness can make us more sympathetic toward others. A person who has never had an ache or pain may not feel too much compassion for sick folks. Just remember: you may be looking down today at someone on a hospital bed, but tomorrow you could be the one on the bed.

4. Can sickness be a punishment? Yes, but not always. Don't look for this every time. It will make you harsh and self-righteous toward others. And it will keep you uptight if you're the sick one. Miriam, Moses' sister, was punished with leprosy (Numbers 12:10). Others in the Bible were also afflicted because of sin. But when Jesus' disciples asked if a man

was blind because of his sin or that of his parents, Jesus answered, "Neither" (John 9:1-3).

We must be very careful not to judge people who are sick. Unfortunately, some have taught that if one is sick it is a sure sign that he has sinned. The apostle Paul left one of his fellow workers, Trophimus, behind him on one trip because he was sick. Paul says nothing to indicate that the man was being punished for sin. Nor does he criticize him for lack of faith (2 Timothy 4:20).

Can Satan afflict a person physically? Yes. Job is a good example (Job 2:7). But remember that the devil was restricted by God as to how far he could go with this (Job 2:6).

When you're in good health it is easy to say that if a person trusts and obeys God fully he will not be sick. Better be careful about such presumption. There are mysteries about God's dealings with us. For some things we may never find an explanation. This is true of sickness. Instead of trying to figure out "why," it is often best simply to commit our ways to the Lord and trust Him to work out His perfect will in us.

## THE SOUL COMES FIRST

"For even hereunto were ye called: because Christ also suffered for us, leaving us an example, that ye should follow his steps: who did no sin, neither was guile found in his mouth: who, when He was reviled, reviled not again; when he suffered, he threatened not, but committed himself to him that judgeth righteously: who his own self bare our sins in his own body on the tree, that we, being dead to sins, should live unto righteousness: by whose stripes ye were healed. For ye were as sheep going astray; but are now returned unto the Shepherd and Bishop of your souls." (1 Peter 2:21-25).

God is interested in both the spiritual and physical welfare of us all. The spiritual part must always come first. Our bodies will die, but out spirits will not. It does little good to have a strong body and a sick soul.

When Jesus died He made an atonement that provides for man's entire being. Thus we have a right to expect physical healing, too. But let's take first things first. We have seen people who were mightily interested in getting well physically, but had little concern about serving God. Pastors are sometimes called to pray for people who declare that if God heals them they will be in church every Sunday. There have been times when God in His mercy *has* healed such people, but not all of these promises have been kept.

The Bible often describes sin as spiritual sickness. David cried, "Heal my soul; for I have sinned against thee" (Psalm 41:4). Isaiah 1:5,6 is a classic passage: "Oh, my people, haven't you had enough of punishment? Why will you force me to whip you again and again? Must you forever rebel? From head to foot you are sick and weak and faint, covered with bruises and welts and infected wounds, unanointed and unbound" (*Living Bible Paraphrased*).

When Jesus began His ministry He went to the synagogue at Nazareth and read from an Old Testament prophecy that referred to Him: "The Spirit of the Lord is upon me, because he hath sent me to heal the broken-hearted, to preach . . . recovering of sight to the blind, to set at liberty them that are bruised" (Luke 4:18).

The sickness of sin has one remedy, and only one.

It is the precious blood of Jesus. Take care of your spiritual needs first. Then you can talk to God about your physical problems.

## "THE LORD FOR THE BODY"

"Now the body is not for fornication, but for the Lord; and the Lord for the body" (1 Corinthians 6: 13). Paul wasn't dealing with divine healing when he wrote those words, but he does state a principle that applies. The Lord is for the body, which surely means that He is concerned about it and can help it when there is a need.

In Jesus' early ministry there was a great scene which Matthew describes like this: "When the even was come, they brought unto him many that were possessed with devils: and he cast out the spirits with his word, and healed all that were sick: That it might be fulfilled which was spoken by Isaiah the prophet, saying, Himself took our infirmities, and bare our sicknesses" (Matthew 8:16,17).

That's quite a picture, isn't it? "Himself bare our sicknesses." Jesus bore our diseases as a burden laid upon Him. When He healed people it was as though He lifted the load of suffering from them and carried it himself.

Jesus came to destroy the works of the devil (1 John 3:8). Sickness came into the world as a result of sin. Satan is the instigator of sin. When our Lord heals sickness it is a foretaste of the day when Satan, sin, and death will all be banished from the scene forever.

God made a promise to the ancient Israelites that included healing as well as deliverance from slavery: "If thou wilt diligently hearken to the voice of the Lord thy God, and wilt do that which is right in his sight, and wilt give ear to his commandments, and keep all his statutes, I will put none of these diseases upon thee, which I have brought upon the Egyptians: for I am the Lord that healeth thee" (Exodus 15:26).

There is a very clear promise in James 5:14,15: "Is any sick among you? let him call for the elders of the church; and let them pray over him, anointing him with oil in the name of the Lord: and the prayer of faith shall save the sick, and the Lord shall raise him up; and if he have committed sins, they shall be forgiven him."

The elders were the spiritual leaders of the church. Often there were several. Today we refer to these leaders as our pastors.

### ONE CAN AFFECT THE OTHER

There is a very short letter in the New Testament which we call Third John. It was written by the apostle John to a Christian named Gaius. The second verse is actually a prayer of the apostle for this man: "Beloved, I wish above all things that thou mayest prosper and be in health, even as thy soul prospereth."

In other words, John's desire for Gaius was that his physical and material well-being would be just as good as his spiritual condition. Obviously Gaius was very healthy spiritually. John says, "May your physical health and your financial state be just as healthy!"

Whether we realize it or not, we are complicated beings. We have spirits, bodies, brains, emotions, and a nervous system. Each human being is such an intricate machine that what affects one part of him affects the others. If we are ill, our mind and nerves soon know it. So does our spirit. There is an interrelationship between spiritual and physical health.

This does not mean that devout Christians will never be sick. And as paradoxical as it seems, ungodly people may enjoy good health. Nevertheless, it is a basic principle that a man's spiritual condition can affect him physically. Undoubtedly many people would recover from what appears to be physical illness, if they would get right spiritually. This applies to unsaved people, but it can also apply to Christians. God's people can get off the track, can't they?

A spiritually healthy Christian will be concerned about remaining healthy physically. He knows his body is God's temple (1 Corinthians 6:19). For this reason he will not be careless about its care. How can it be pleasing to God for His people to disregard all of the rules of health? Sickness may sometimes be the inevitable result of our breaking many of these rules. To maintain spiritual and physical health it is necessary to avoid things that are definitely sinful. It is also necessary to steer clear of things that are harmful to the body. That certainly includes alcohol or tobacco, doesn't it? It includes a lot of other things, too. We're at the end of this chapter, so we don't have space to talk about the whole list. But you are well aware of them, aren't you?

Wouldn't it be great if we could be as concerned about our spiritual health as we are about our bodies. If we were, it would soon react on us physically. Have you tried it?

# 8
# Remember!

### PRECIOUS BLOOD

The cost of redeeming you and me was colossal. It was nothing less than the blood of Jesus Christ. Listen to this: "God paid a ransom to save you from the impossible road to heaven which your fathers tried to take, and the ransom he paid was not mere gold or silver, as you very well know. But he paid for you with the precious lifeblood of Christ, the sinless, spotless, Lamb of God" (1 Peter 1:18,19, *Living Bible Paraphrased*).

What a foundation is to a house the doctrine of Jesus' blood atonement is to the gospel. Remove it, and the whole structure collapses. "It is the blood that maketh an atonement for the soul" is an everlasting principle in God's dealings with man (Leviticus 17:11). "Without shedding of blood is no remission," Hebrews 9:22 declares emphatically.

If Jesus had done no more than come to earth to give us a new set of religious teachings, the world would no doubt have been helped, but it would not have been redeemed. It took His death to do that. This is why He came at all. He looked forward to the Cross from the moment He arrived on this planet of ours.

John 3:16 has been called the golden text of the Bible: "For God so loved the world, that he gave his only begotten Son, that whosoever believeth in him should not perish, but have everlasting life." In what sense did God give His Son? Not only by sending Him to the world, but by sending Him to His death. Never forget that this was at a terrible cost to the Father as well as the Son. Would you give up your son to save someone who hated you and tried to do you all the harm he could?

It is no wonder the Bible calls the shed blood of Christ "precious." When something is precious it is very costly; of untold value. Every Christian cries "Amen" when he hears the blood of Jesus called "precious." And he staggers back in awe when he says it.

In our commercial world a lot of stain-removers are on the market. The greatest stain of all is the one left on the human life by sin. And the only remover is this precious Blood. The stain is too deep for anything human to do the job.

## JESUS COMMANDED IT

When Jesus was about to go to the Cross He had one last meal with His disciples. That particular meal was the Jewish Passover. It was a feast of remembrance. God had commanded the Jews to observe it every year so they would always be reminded of their deliverance from Egypt. The greatest feature of that deliverance was the manner in which the Jewish firstborn were spared from death. It happened because each family sprinkled a lamb's blood on the door of their home.

After Jesus and His disciples finished eating the Passover meal He instituted what we call the Lord's Supper. It was a good background for those Jewish disciples. They had just been reminded again that their ancestors were freed from slavery by the blood of an unblemished lamb. That lamb was a picture of Jesus Christ, whom John the Baptist called "the Lamb of God" (John 1:29).

"And he took bread, and gave thanks, and brake it, and gave unto them, saying, This is my body which is given for you: this do in remembrance of me. Likewise also the cup after supper, saying, This cup is the new testament in my blood, which is shed for you" (Luke 22:19,20).

Jesus' death marked the dividing line between God's old covenant (testament) with men, and His new one. Men had been living under the old covenant, the Law. That was to be superseded by a new covenant, the gospel of Jesus Christ. Atoning blood was the basis of the old covenant. It was the blood of animals. They were constantly being sacrificed for the people's sins. Such sacrifices could not atone for sins permanently, so there had to be many of them. It was a temporary arrangement God made with men until Jesus came.

The new covenant is not based on the blood of animals, but on the blood of God's Son. His sacrifice never has to be repeated because it is perfect.

Jesus often spoke symbolically. He said He was the true Vine. He called himself the Bread of Life. Such expressions were obviously figurative. When He said the bread and the wine were His body and His blood He did not mean that these elements actually become His body and blood when we take Communion. They are symbols; pictures. If they literally became His body and blood, this would mean that Christ would be sacrificed again at every Communion service. Such a thought is not only abhorrent, but completely unscriptural.

## THE APOSTLES OBEYED HIM

We rightfully call the Lord's Supper an ordinance of the Church. An ordinance is something ordained. Jesus himself ordained the Lord's Supper, or Communion.

The apostle Paul was not present in the Upper Room, but he gave us some wonderful teaching about the Last Supper:

"The Lord Jesus the same night in which He was betrayed took bread. And when He had given thanks He brake it and said, Take, eat. This is my Body, which is broken for you. This do in remembrance of Me.

"After the same manner also he took the cup, when he had supped, saying, This cup is the new testament in my blood: this do ye, as oft as ye drink it, in remembrance of me. For as often as ye eat this bread, and drink this cup, ye do show the Lord's death till he come" (1 Corinthians 11:25,26).

On that night before He died, Jesus observed the Lord's Supper with His disciples. It drew them all together in a closer fellowship as Christ neared the Cross. Jesus did not intend that the Lord's Supper should be a one-time-only observance. It was to be repeated many, many times. "This do" means "keep on doing this" (Luke 22:19; 1 Corinthians 11:24,25).

In Acts 2:46 we are told that the first Christians continued "breaking bread from house to house." This was undoubtedly a reference to their constant observance of the Lord's Supper. In Acts 2:42 we read that from the Day of Pentecost onward "they continued steadfastly in the apostles' doctrine and fel-

lowship, and in breaking of bread, and in prayers."
This "breaking of bread," then, became a part of the
doctrine of the Early Church.

Apparently Paul received his knowledge of the
Lord's Supper by a direct revelation from the Lord
Jesus. His testimony was "I received of the Lord" (1
Corinthians 11:23). That Paul got his knowledge in
this manner indicates how important the Lord must
consider His Supper to be.

Paul was just as aware of the significance of this
ordinance as the other disciples. He knew that the
entire observance symbolized the death of Christ as
a substitute for sinners. He was careful and emphatic in teaching Christians to keep observing this
Supper.

The Lord's Supper is frequently called "Communion." This speaks of our sharing, or participating in,
the benefits of Christ's atonement. Some call it the
Eucharist because the Greek word for "thanks" is
*eucharistesas*. Jesus, you will remember, gave thanks
as He passed the bread and cup to His disciples.

## It's Still for the Church

The apostles not only received the ordinance of the
Lord's Supper themselves. They also received it to
transmit to the church. All believers should observe
it. They should be very conscious of its meaning as
they do so.

The meaning of the Lord's Supper is the same today as it was in the early days of the church. When
a Christian takes Communion he is looking back at
the way Christ died as a substitute for him. It is a
time of remembrance, as Jesus intended it to be: "This
do in remembrance of me."

We should also remember what our end would

have been if we had not met and accepted Christ. It's a terrible thought, but it's good for us to consider it occasionally.

The Lord's Supper has always been a great unifying force in the church. "The cup of blessing which we bless, is it not the communion of the blood of Christ? The bread which we break, is it not the communion of the body of Christ? For we being many are one bread, and one body: for we are all partakers of that one bread" (1 Corinthians 10:16,17).

No matter who we are, each one of us has to come to God the same way. We are saved by the blood of Jesus, or we are not saved at all. When we gather around the Lord's table we represent all kinds of backgrounds, temperaments, and personalities. But as we eat the bread and drink of the cup we all become one in Christ.

The Communion table reminds us also of the necessity of our being separated from the world and its sins. "Ye cannot drink the cup of the Lord, and the cup of devils: ye cannot be partakers of the Lord's table, and of the table of devils" (1 Corinthians 10:21).

Christians must live in this world until the Lord calls them home. But while in the world physically they must not be a part of it spiritually and morally. The devil is in control of the majority of humans on this planet. Those who are saved by Jesus' blood must be different. They must be pure and holy. Nothing presses this home to us more forcefully than those moments we are at the Lord's table.

Some churches observe Communion more frequently than others. It is not good to have too long a span of time between Communion services. Our memories need to be stimulated often concerning the cost of our redemption. We need the spiritual strength that comes when we think of Calvary again.

## ANTICIPATION

Paul's teaching introduces another element into the Lord's Supper. He says it is not only a time of looking back, but of looking forward. "For as often as ye eat this bread, and drink this cup, ye do show the Lord's death till he come" (1 Corinthians 11:26).

Before He was crucified, Jesus talked about His second coming. This is not a cold theological doctrine. It is a bright, exhilarating hope. Every Communion service brings us that much closer to the glorious hour of His return.

God's plan of redemption has a time limit. Jesus said He came to build a church (Matthew 16:18). Just as every building program comes to its climax, so will the building of the church. When it is finished, Jesus will come again.

In our observance of the Lord's Supper we are reminded that our salvation cost God tremendously. We are also reminded that the Lord's cause will be victorious. Sin may have the upper hand today, but that will end when Jesus comes as King of kings and Lord of lords.

## TESTIMONY

"Ye do show the Lord's death" means "You proclaim the Lord's death." Thus the Lord's Supper is a time of testimony. When we partake of it we are witnessing to the fact that we believe the gospel. It tells everyone who sees us that we have accepted the crucified Christ as our Lord and Saviour.

This is another reason Christians should not neglect the Lord's Supper. It is not a take-it-or-leave-it proposition. It is a divine command. It is another way to spread the message. No matter how timid we are about testifying, we can take Communion. When we do, we are saying, "I believe Jesus died for my sins and for the sins of the whole world."

Is it a good testimony to the unsaved for Christians to walk nonchalantly out of church while others are going to the Lord's table? Is it so important to get home to watch that game on television that we treat the Saviour's command this way? Is anything so important as telling the world of His death on Calvary? That death is not only to be proclaimed from the pulpit, but from the Communion table—by every participating believer. It is not merely an opportunity and privilege, but a duty. We are the worse if we ignore it.

## Watch Your Attitude

In Paul's teaching about the Lord's Supper there are a number of warnings. In fact he scolded the Corinthians severely for some of the things they were doing at Communion. We are not to partake in a careless or unworthy manner, for these elements represent the sacrifice of Christ for sinners.

"Wherefore whosoever shall eat this bread, and drink this cup of the Lord, unworthily, shall be guilty of the body and blood of the Lord. But let a man examine himself, and so let him eat of that bread, and drink of that cup. For he that eateth and drinketh unworthily, eateth and drinketh damnation to himself, not discerning the Lord's body. For this cause many are weak and sickly among you, and many sleep. For if we would judge ourselves, we should not be judged. But when we are judged, we are chastened of the Lord, that we should not be condemned with the world" (1 Corinthians 11:27-32).

The Lord's Supper is a time of self-examination. It is a solemn occasion during which the Christian should put himself to the test. When Paul speaks of drinking "damnation" to one's self he uses a Greek word referring to a temporary judgment that is intended to save an individual rather than destroy him. When he speaks of being condemned with the world his word for "condemned" refers to the final judgment. Some of the temporary punishment coming on the Corinthians was physical affliction. There can be other punishments, of course, besides sickness.

Much of the Corinthians' problems seemed to stem from actual irreverence. In those days the Christians had a full meal together when they took Communion. Some were using this as a time of revelry and gluttony. Some were even getting drunk (1 Corinthians 11:21).

It is not likely that we will go this far in any unworthy partaking of Communion. But we still must be sure that we come very reverently to the Lord's table. There must be no frivolity nor lightness. Hatred, jealousy, an unforgiving spirit—these and other inward attitudes should be dealt with quickly when we are coming to eat the bread and drink the cup.

Attitude is an important thing in the Christian life. This is especially true at the Communion table. The Lord looks on our hearts. Let's be sure He always sees what He wants to see, and not something that grieves Him.

# 9
# Called Out

"Called out." That's the meaning of the Greek word used for "church" in the New Testament (*ekklésia*). It's exactly what the Church is all about. We're talking, of course, about what is sometimes called "the invisible church." This is made up of all born-again believers, regardless of denomination. We'll be discussing the visible church, too, a bit farther on.

A person becomes a member of this invisible Church when he is called out by the Spirit of God from the sins of the world around him. Naturally he is not called out in the sense of leaving this planet. But he is called out from the philosophy, morals, motives, life-style, and sin of the human race. The Bible says the Christian is "separated." His salvation draws an unseen line between him and those who are not believers.

Members of different denominations can enjoy fellowship with each other when both are true Christians. They are both called out. They are members of one Church even though their earthly memberships are in different organizations. As we shall point out later, church membership is desirable, but belonging to the invisible Church must come first. If that membership is missing, all of the church-joining one might do will be of no avail.

Jesus himself mentioned the word "church" first in the New Testament. He said He came to build what He called "my church" (Matthew 16:18). This building started on the Day of Pentecost, as recorded in Acts 2. At first it was nearly all Jewish, but later the Gentiles began to come in. The Bible makes it clear that the true Church will be composed of people from every race, culture, and nation (Revelation 5:9). We say "true" Church because there is also a false church. There are religious organizations operating under the name of "church" which deny the foundation truths of the gospel. Naturally the members of such churches can have no real spiritual life. This is why it is so important to understand what the Church really is. To some people, joining a church is synonymous with being a Christian, but the Bible does not support this.

Aside from the Gospels and Acts, the whole New Testament is a collection of letters to churches, or to key persons in churches.

### The Foundation Is Unshakable

When Jesus said He would "build" His Church, the figure of a building was immediately suggested. Buildings, if they are to stand, must have strong foundations. The Church's foundation is the strongest.

"And I say unto thee, that thou art Peter, and upon this rock I will build my church, and the gates of hell shall not prevail against it" (Matthew 16:18).

Those are the words of Jesus. To understand them we must know what had just taken place. Jesus had asked His disciples what people were saying about Him. There was a variety of answers. Some reported that Jesus was believed to be a resurrected John the Baptist. Others thought He was Elijah, Jeremiah, or another prophet. The important thing to Jesus was what His disciples thought about Him. Peter gave the answer: "Thou are the Christ, the Son of the living God" (Matthew 16:16). Jesus immediately told Peter that this knowledge had come to him by divine revelation. Then followed our Lord's statement about building His Church.

It was Peter's confession of faith that revealed the foundation upon which Jesus could build His Church. Peter himself was not that foundation. The words "Peter" and "rock" are different words in the Greek New Testament. "Peter" is a translation of the Greek word *petros,* which means "stone." "Rock" is a translation of the Greek word *petra,* which means solid bedrock. The use of these two distinctively different words shows that Jesus did not intend to build His Church on Peter.

Christ purposed to build a Church, but it could not be built upon a foundation of men—even *good* men. At best, these men of God could be but stones. Jesus Christ himself is the bedrock upon which His Church is built. Peter was not the foundation rock of the Church. He was a stone in the structure, just as you and I are. We become stones the same way Peter did—by our belief and confession that Jesus is the Christ, the Son of the living God.

"For through him we both have access by one Spirit unto the Father. Now therefore ye are no more strangers and foreigners, but fellow citizens with the saints, and of the household of God; and are built upon the foundation of the apostles and prophets, Jesus Christ himself being the chief corner stone" (Ephesians 2:18-20).

The chief cornerstone was a large foundation stone which joined two walls, uniting them and bearing their weight. What a description of Jesus!

## THERE'S A PLACE FOR ALL

The Bible pictures the Church not only as a building of which Christ is the foundation, but also as a body of which He is the Head. Christians are not only living stones in a building; they are parts of a body.

The Church is the spiritual body of Christ. He is "head of the body, the church" (Colossians 1:18). God the Father "gave him to be head over all things to the church, which is his body, the fulness of him that filleth all in all" (Ephesians 1:22,23). "The church is subject unto Christ" (Ephesians 5:24) because "Christ is the head of the church: and he is the saviour of the body" (Ephesians 5:23).

People become members of the true Church by accepting Christ as Saviour. Here is what Paul told one congregation: "For as the body is one, and hath many members, and all the members of that one body, being many, are one body: so also is Christ. For by one Spirit are we all baptized into one body, whether we be Jews or Gentiles, whether we be bond or free; and have been all made to drink into one Spirit. For the body is not one member, but many. Now ye are the body of Christ, and members in particular" (1 Corinthians 12:12-14,27).

The human body is a marvelous structure. Can you do without any part of it? Sometimes we lose parts and have to get along as best we can, but it is not easy. That little finger may not seem important until it is cut off.

Paul says it's the same in the Church. God himself is the designer of the human body. He has also designed the Church. Our body has parts that enable it to see, hear, think, move, taste, talk, and perform the other duties of living. Every joint, ligament, nerve, blood vessel, and tendon has a function.

Some of our body parts seem more prominent than others, but this does not mean that the less prominent parts are unnecessary. Don't ever let yourself think, "No one will miss me if I'm not in church." That's just like your toe or ear or finger thinking it wouldn't be missed! If you are not functioning properly the body, the Church, will not be at its best.

As a member of Christ's body you are dear to Him. He has paid a tremendous price for you—His own blood. No Christian needs to have an inferiority complex. Belonging to Christ is the greatest thing that can happen to you. Being just a small part of His body is an honor.

### KEEP THAT BODY HEALTHY!

Who wants to drag a sick body around? Sometimes we have to, but we do our best to recover as soon as possible.

And who wants a sick church? A body is made up of members, and so is a church. If a church is sick, the disease is in its members!

Proper functioning of the body means that every member of the body is in its right place, performing its proper task. "If the foot shall say, Because I am not the hand, I am not of the body; is it therefore not of the body? And if the ear shall say, Because I am not the eye, I am not of the body; is it therefore not of the body? If the whole body were an eye, where were the hearing? If the whole were hearing, where were the smelling?" (1 Corinthians 12:15-17).

Members of a body bear a relationship to each other. Hands and feet must often coordinate their work. When the individual parts of the body get out of harmony with each other, there is sickness and weakness.

It is just as true in the Church. We are not isolated. Each member is related to the others. The foot cannot try to take over the functions of the whole body without causing disaster. It has its place, but it is not the whole body. It must consider the other members. So must we as members of Christ's body.

The place each member of the body of Christ occupies in that body is dependent upon God and His will. It does not depend on the desires of the members. "But now hath God set the members every one of them in the body, as it hath pleased him" (1 Corinthians 12:18). Each member is assigned to the position and function in which he can best work for the welfare of the whole body. That is why, for example, the Holy Spirit has bestowed different spiritual gifts upon different members of the Church. God knows which members of the Church can best exercise which gifts for the good of all (1 Corinthians 12:12).

Regular Bible study and prayer are essential to the health of each member of Christ's body. So is consistent church attendance and worship. So is faithful service. Learning self-discipline is extremely important. We must control our tongues. We must keep our minds clean. There are so many things to be said about maintaining our spiritual health that it would fill a lot of space if we tried to talk about them all.

ORGANIZATION? DEFINITELY!

Sometimes people who have come out of churches that are highly organized but spiritually dead have declared, "No more organization for me!" This, of course, is not scriptural.

"And we beseech you, brethren, to know them which labor among you, and are over you in the Lord, and admonish you; and to esteem them very highly in love for their work's sake. And be at peace among yourselves" (1 Thessalonians 5:12,13).

We have been talking about the human body as a picture of the Church. Would anyone dare to say the body is not organized? On the contrary, it is a *model* of organization. If it were not, we would fall on our faces each time we tried to take a step.

The church had organization even in its early days. The first evidence was in the Upper Room when a successor to Judas was chosen (Acts 1:15-26).

The church grew so rapidly that problems soon developed. One of the first was the distribution of food to widows. To take care of this, deacons had to be selected (Acts 6:17). As more local churches sprang into being, they had their own bishops and deacons (Philippians 1:1).

The word "bishop" means "overseer," just like the Greek work *episkopos,* which it translates. The function of a bishop was to "oversee" a local church. They were also called elders (compare Acts 20:17,28). They were the pastors, or shepherds, of the local churches. "Take heed therefore unto yourselves, and to all the flock, over the which the Holy Ghost hath made you overseers, to feed the church of God, which he hath purchased with his own blood" (Acts 20:28). The office of bishop, or pastor, is an honorable one (1 Timothy 5:1,17-19). Because of its high honor there are strict qualifications for the office (1 Timothy 3:1-7; Titus 1:5-9).

The office of deacon is also an honorable one, with strict qualifications (Acts 6:3; 1 Timothy 3:8-13). Our word "deacon" is really the Greek word *diakonos* (servant), which we have borrowed and made a part of our language. Deacons were added to the organization of the church to free those exercising pastoral ministry from the cares of the temporal affairs of the church. Deacons were appointed to "serve tables" so the spiritual overseers could devote themselves to prayer and the ministry of the Word (Acts 6:1-6). Since the word "tables" in Acts 6:2 means "money tables," we infer that the financial affairs of the church were in the hands of the deacons.

Although the organization of the Early Church was somewhat flexible in order to meet changing needs and conditions, certain principles are observable in it. These principles are just as sound and spiritual today as then.

## Is Membership Important?

The answer to the above question is a loud "Yes!" It may sound very spiritual to declare, "I'm a member of Christ's church. I don't belong to any earthly church." But such a philosophy is very shortsighted. It is also quite self-righteous.

Church membership should be very meaningful. It is regrettable that much laxity prevails in many churches, which seem to have no membership standards. It seems a tragedy that while many lodges and fraternal organizations have rather strict regulations about joining, there is a feeling in many quarters that it is wrong to erect any kind of standards for the church.

Since formal membership in the church gives an individual the privilege of helping elect its ministers and officers and set its policies, it seems only logical that members should be in agreement with the church's doctrines and practices. Some have rebelled against making such a commitment. Others, for some reason, have not joined a church because they do not wish to be baptized in water. It must be remembered that water baptism is our Lord's own clear command (Matthew 28:19).

Some have thought that since church membership does not save, such membership is unnecessary. One sometimes wonders, however, if this is only an excuse to escape responsibility. Being a church member does involve responsibility, you know.

The local church is the battleground on which the spiritual warfare of this age has always been fought. There were local churches in New Testament times. Those churches had members. They had leaders. They were united in a common purpose. They were not a mob straggling along to nowhere. They had rules and regulations. They strove together to obey the same Lord.

Joining a church and giving it your spiritual and financial support will strengthen your own Christian life. Being united with other Christians in the membership of a Bible-based, Christ-exalting church gives one a sense of stability and security in these stormy times.

# 10
# God's Business Managers

## NOTHING IS REALLY OURS

The Bible uses the word *steward* a number of times. A steward was a business manager for a wealthy man. The money and property he handled were not his. They belonged to the man he worked for, and he was responsible to him for every penny.

If a steward started thinking it was his own wealth he was managing and began treating it that way, he didn't last long. From time to time there had to be an accounting with his boss.

According to the New Testament, every Christian is a steward of God—accountable to Him for that stewardship. He is a manager of the earthly goods God has committed to his care. He is responsible for the way in which he uses what has been entrusted to him.

Christian stewardship is based on two fundamental facts. Both involve the believer's relationship to God. First, everything a Christian possesses comes from God. Read these passages very carefully: Matthew 6:22-34; 2 Corinthians 9:8; Deuteronomy 8:11-18. Second, everything a Christian has should be consecrated to God. If the individual is thoroughly dedicated to the Lord, his possessions will be dedicated, too. Read 2 Corinthians 8:5.

Money is a touchy subject. Fortunately we have some very clear Scripture on the matter. Since money is such an important part of life, it's not surprising that the Bible has something to say about it. First, let's look at 2 Corinthians 9:5-8, *Living Bible Paraphrased*:

"So I have asked these other brothers to arrive ahead of me to see that the gift you promised is on hand and waiting. I want it to be a real gift and not look as if it were being given under pressure. But remember this—if you give little, you will get little. A farmer who plants just a few seeds will get only a small crop, but if he plants much, he will reap much. Every one must make up his own mind as to how much he should give. Don't force anyone to give more than he really wants to, for cheerful givers are the ones God prizes. God is able to make it up to you by giving you everything you need and more, so that there will not only be enough for your own needs, but plenty left over to give joyfully to others."

Paul was collecting money for the Christians at Jerusalem. This passage is a part of his instructions about this collection. It contains some excellent principles that should govern all of our giving. The main thing to remember is that what we have is actually God's. We are managing it just like the Biblical steward. And we will answer to Him for the way we do it.

## DON'T BE A FOOL

God warned the Israelites against forgetting that He was the source of their possessions: "When thou hast eaten and art full, then thou shalt bless the Lord thy God for the good land which he hath given thee. Beware that thou forget not the Lord thy God, in not keeping his commandments, and His judgments, and

93

his statutes, which I command thee this day: lest when thou hast eaten and art full, and hast built goodly houses, and dwelt therein; and when thy herds and thy flocks multiply, and thy silver and thy gold is multiplied, and all that thou hast is multiplied; then thine heart be lifted up, and thou forget the Lord thy God, which brought thee forth out of the land of Egypt, from the house of bondage . . . and thou say in thine heart, My power and the might of mine hand hath gotten me this wealth. But thou shalt remember the Lord thy God, for it is he that giveth thee power to get wealth, that he may establish his covenant which he sware unto thy fathers, as it is this day" ( Deuteronomy 8:10-14,17,18).

Israel failed to heed God's warnings and was punished for it. When prosperity smiles on a man it is all too easy for him to forget the God who is responsible for his good fortune.

Jesus once told a story about a rich man who forgot that his wealth came from God, and refused to consider himself as a steward of the Lord: "The ground of a certain rich man brought forth plentifully: and he thought within himself, saying, What shall I do, because I have no room where to bestow my fruits? And he said, This will I do: I will pull down my barns, and build greater; and there will I bestow all my fruits and my goods. And I will say to my soul, Soul, thou hast much goods laid up for many years; take thine ease, eat, drink, and be merry" ( Luke 12:16-19).

Did you notice how many times the pronouns *I* and *my* occur in that parable? The man is a picture of self-centered satisfaction. He believed that the things committed to his care were actually his own. He was saying in his heart, "My power and the might of mine hand hath gotten me this wealth" (Deuteronomy 8: 17). He had forgotten God. He refused to consider himself the steward of God.

But God is not so easily set aside. Here's what happened after the man's conversation with himself: "But God said unto him, Thou fool, this night thy soul shall be required of thee: then whose shall those things be, which thou hast provided?" (Luke 12:20).

Did you hear it? God called him a fool. Sorry to say, he was not the *last* fool that ever lived. Don't you be another! The man who thinks he owns everything really owns nothing; not even his own life. God will eventually take back even that life.

## RESIST THE PULL!

It's pretty hard to argue with the statement that this age is highly materialistic. The majority are preoccupied with material things, and place little value on the spiritual. Financial security is not evil in itself, but when it becomes the dominant goal of life, this is tragic.

Keeping up with the Joneses has been the downfall of many. Too many folks are living far outside their incomes in order to make a good showing to those around them. Easy credit has pulled multitudes into financial waters that are over their heads. The reason some Christians say, "I can't pay my tithes" is that they have splurged so much they don't have enough money to go around. So God gets left out!

It's all too easy to get caught up in this whirl. We are an affluent nation. We have always had not only enough, but more than enough. It takes strong Christian character to keep our balance. Perhaps we should keep these words of Jesus pasted on our bathroom mirror where we can read them every day:

"You cannot serve two masters: God and money.

For you will hate one and love the other, or else the other way around.

"So my counsel is: Don't worry about *things*—food, drink, and clothes. For you already have life and a body—and they are far more important than what to eat and wear. Look at the birds! They don't worry about what to eat—they don't need to sow or reap or store up food—for your heavenly Father feeds them. And you are far more valuable to him than they are. Will all your worries add a single moment to your life?

"And why worry about your clothes? Look at the field lilies! They don't worry about theirs. Yet King Solomon in all his glory was not clothed as beautifully as they. And if God cares so wonderfully for flowers that are here today and gone tomorrow, won't he more surely care for you, O men of little faith?

"So don't worry at all about having enough food and clothing. Why be like the heathen? For they take pride in all these things and are deeply concerned about them. But your heavenly Father already knows perfectly well that you need them, and he will give them to you if you give him first place in your life and live as he wants you to.

"So don't be anxious about tomorrow. God will take care of your tomorrow too. Live one day at a time" (Matthew 6:24-34, *Living Bible Paraphrased*).

As Christians we must keep the right balance between legitimate ambition and spiritual dedication. We must make money our servant; never our master. To let it master us is to become what the Bible labels "worldly."

### WHO WOULD WANT TO DO LESS?

The Lord Jesus was a faithful steward. He was dedicated even in the use of His life. "For ye know the grace of our Lord Jesus Christ, that, though he was rich, yet for your sakes he became poor, that ye through his poverty might be rich" (2 Corinthians 8:9).

Christ gave liberally. He divested himself of His glory (John 17:5; Hebrews 1:3). He emptied himself of His equality of relationship with the Father, and ultimately gave His very life (Philippians 2:5-8).

With such an example before us as the life of our Lord, who would want to give Him anything less than his best? Shall we hold everything selfishly for personal interests when He gave us everything He had? Can we rightfully claim to be His followers if we are stingy, tightfisted, and selfish?

Paul wanted the Corinthian Christians to be good stewards. That is why he urged them to give regularly: "Upon the first day of the week let every one of you lay by him in store, as God hath prospered him" (1 Corinthians 16:2).

To practice tithing as a minimum in giving is undoubtedly the best way to give "as God hath prospered." The question is often asked, "Wasn't tithing just for those under the Law?" While tithing was practiced under the Law, it was also practiced before the Law was given. Melchizedek received tithes from Abraham (Hebrews 7:6). When Jesus came He pointed out that the Pharisees, among other things, were very careful to pay their tithes. In Matthew 5: 20 He said, "Except your righteousness shall exceed the righteousness of the scribes and Pharisees, ye shall in no case enter into the kingdom of heaven." People under grace will certainly not want to give less to the Lord than people under the Law!

In case you have any question about the meaning

of the word *tithe,* it is one-tenth. A tither is one who gives the Lord at least one-tenth of his income.

As God gives to the Christian, that person, being a steward, or business manager, gives back to God. Listen to Paul again in 2 Corinthians 8:11,12, *Living Bible Paraphrased*: "Having started the ball rolling so enthusiastically, you should carry this project through to completion just as gladly, giving whatever you can out of whatever you have. Let your enthusiastic idea at the start be equalled by your realistic action now. If you are really eager to give, then it isn't important how much you have to give. God wants you to give what you have, not what you haven't."

And here's another verse: "Every man according as he purposeth in his heart, so let him give; not grudgingly, or of necessity, for God loveth a cheerful giver" (2 Corinthians 9:7).

So we can't use the excuse that we don't make enough to tithe. God holds us responsible for what we have, not for what we don't have. And if we are to reap the greatest blessing we must see to it that our giving is joyful. If it is only because of pressure or arm-twisting it certainly will not do our spirits much good.

## MULTIPLIED SEED

"Now he that ministereth seed to the sower both minister bread for your food, and multiply your seed sown, and increase the fruits of your righteousness: being enriched in every thing to all bountifulness, which causeth through us thanksgiving to God. For the administration of this service not only supplieth the want of the saints, but is abundant also by many thanksgivings unto God; while by the experiment of this ministration they glorify God for your professed subjection unto the gospel of Christ, and for your liberal distribution unto them, and unto all men" (2 Corinthians 9:10-13).

The farmer knows that bountiful sowing results in bountiful reaping. The harvest is proportional to the seed sown. This is just as true spiritually as in the harvest of wheat and corn.

"And God is able to make all grace abound toward you; that ye, always having all sufficiency in all things, may abound to every good work" (2 Corinthians 9:8). To those who give, God gives back.

There are spiritual rewards for good stewardship. The giver is favored with the love of God in a special way: "For God loveth a cheerful giver." Being faithful in giving keeps our conscience clear, too!

Good stewardship is a form of Christian service. The one who is not called to preach, or go to a foreign field, or even teach a Sunday school class, can still put his money to work for God. This is an area of Christian service in which every believer may share.

Good stewardship is a testimony that the giver is a participant in the grace of God. Cheerful giving is a witness that grace has been received from God. "Freely ye have received, freely give" (Matthew 10:8). All Christians should be good givers. Giving is an enriching experience.

The stingy individual often finds that instead of having more, he has less. It has often been said, "You can't outgive God." Liberal givers can say a loud "Amen" to that! It's a principle that has been tried and proved over and over.

## IT TAKES DETERMINATION

Stewardship is not an option. It is a command, and a necessity. True spirituality and financial giving have

99

always gone hand in hand. The handling of money is the acid test of character. Some Christians who have done well in other areas have failed in this one.

Doing anything worth while in life takes determination. Tithing takes a lot of it. A person who has never practiced tithing may grow panicky at the thought of taking out one-tenth of his income before he spends any on himself. He may look at those bills and say, "I can't get along with nine-tenths! I need ten-tenths, and even more!" But multitudes of tithers could rise up and testify that God has a miraculous way of making the nine-tenths go farther than the ten-tenths.

More self-discipline is probably required in the management of money than any other realm. It takes real determination to take out the Lord's tenth every payday before making any personal expenditures. Someone has well said that God is our first creditor. We must take the position that we have a bill we must pay the Lord out of each paycheck just as we do our car payments and all the others. Let's get with it!

# 11
# Jesus Said "Go"

The world is in terrible shape! And it's getting worse.

The earliest members of the human race knew all about God. Gradually, but deliberately, they turned away from their Creator. When this began to happen, each succeeding generation knew less about God than the one before. This is why Christians must go! When we talk about missionary work we're talking about restoring the knowledge of God to those who have lost it.

Every Christian is called to go. Not everyone is called to give his entire time to active missionary work, but all can give and all can pray. Those who do not leave their secular jobs must be faithful supporters of Christ's missionary program for reaching the multitudes.

"The field is the world." Those are Jesus' own words in Matthew 13:38. We often apply this only to foreign countries. But our own nation is part of the world. So is our neighborhood. There is spiritual need everywhere. There is no way for God's people to escape their responsibility to all men without Christ.

A missionary is a person sent on a mission. We

might use the word *errand.* The need for missionaries is as old as sin and the need for salvation. Whenever and wherever man has sinned he needs to be told about Christ. That includes your next-door neighbor as well as the heathen abroad.

Let's hear a little of what the Bible says about man's downward slide into more and more sin. In Romans 1:22,23, *Living Bible Paraphrased,* Paul describes men of old who turned from God: "Claiming themselves to be wise without God, they became utter fools instead. And then, instead of worshiping the glorious, ever-living God, they took wood and stone and made idols for themselves, carving them to look like mere birds and animals and snakes and puny men."

This passage, of course, speaks of idol worship. There is something in man's nature that makes it necessary for him to worship something. Many have made their own gods out of wood, stone, and metal. Naturally, civilized people don't do this now. But that doesn't mean idolatry has ended. An idol is *anything* that takes God's place in a human life.

Certainly it is not a distortion to say that all men outside of Christ are idolaters. Their idols may be different from those of old, but they have set something else up in the place of God. This is why we must go, and go, and go. There is no end to our work because there is no end to sin. We must teach men to give God first place in their lives instead of second, or third, or *last* place.

## THE FIRST MISSIONARY

There is no doubt about it; Jesus Christ was God's first missionary. He came to this lost world on a mission. That mission was not merely to give us a new set of rules to live by. He did more than live a great life. He came to deal with the sin problem. And this meant giving himself completely; even dying.

Jesus said, "I must work the works of him that sent me, while it is day: the night cometh, when no man can work" (John 9:4). Sometime when you are reading the Gospels please notice how many times our Lord used the word "must." Every day of His earthly life He felt the urgency of His mission. He was driven by it. It occupied His thoughts day and night. Satan tried to turn Him away from His goal when he tempted Him in the wilderness. But Jesus flung these temptations away and moved on toward the Cross. He would not be stopped, even by Satan.

Jesus said, "For the Son of man is come to seek and to save that which was lost" (Luke 19:10). He related stories about a lost sheep and a lost son and a lost coin (Luke 15). He told of the urgency of the shepherd in looking for the lost sheep. He talked about how earnestly a person will search even for a piece of money that has been lost in the house. And He pictured a father running down the road to meet a wayward son. These illustrations, or parables, reveal the very heart of God. No shepherd, no earthly father, could possess even a fraction of the compassion that Jesus felt about finding human beings who are spiritually lost.

Missionaries who preach on foreign soil leave comfortable homes. They bid farewell to their native land. Jesus did more. He left heaven. Foreign missionaries often go where the climate, food, and other conditions are unpleasant. But Jesus left His heavenly home where there was no sin, sorrow, sickness, or death. He came to a degraded world where such things abound.

Even when Jesus was still a boy He asked His

mother and Joseph, "Wist ye not that I must be about my Father's business?" (Luke 2:49). There's that "must"—even before He began His actual ministry.

## ORDERS FROM THE COMMANDER IN CHIEF

"Go ye therefore, and teach all nations, baptizing them in the name of the Father, and of the Son, and of the Holy Ghost: teaching them to observe all things whatsoever I have commanded you: and, lo, I am with you alway, even unto the end of the world" (Matthew 28:19,20).

Those words come from none less than the head of the Church. They are the command of Jesus Christ himself. Who could get orders from any higher source?

After His resurrection Jesus commanded His disciples to become missionaries. He opened the Scriptures so they could understand what they must preach: "Thus it is written, and thus it behooved Christ to suffer, and to rise from the dead the third day: and that repentance and remission of sins should be preached in his name among all nations, beginning at Jerusalem. And ye are witnesses of these things" (Luke 24:46-48).

Jesus not only commanded His disciples; He empowered them: "And, behold, I send the promise of my Father upon you: but tarry ye in the city of Jerusalem, until ye be endued with power from on high" (Luke 24:49). Just before His ascension He promised, "But ye shall receive power, after that the Holy Ghost is come upon you: and ye shall be witnesses unto me" (Acts 1:8). Before they could be effective witnesses they must be baptized in the Holy Spirit. So must we!

The Lord also promised to confirm the word His disciples preached. He would do this, He said, with "signs." "And these signs shall follow them that believe: In my name shall they cast out devils; they shall speak with new tongues; they shall take up serpents; and if they drink any deadly thing, it shall not hurt them; they shall lay hands on the sick, and they shall recover. So then, after the Lord had spoken unto them, he was received up into heaven, and sat on the right hand of God. And they went forth, and preached everywhere, the Lord working with them, and confirming the word with signs following" (Mark 16:17-20).

Those signs were God's way of telling the world that what the disciples preached about Jesus was true. He still confirms His Word with signs following. His miraculous power was not displayed only in the first century. It will continue until Jesus comes back for His Church.

Although the disciples were to go into all the world, Jesus told them they must begin at Jerusalem. Then they were to move out into Judea, Samaria, and finally the uttermost part of the earth (Acts 1:8). The first missionary activity was to be home missions. Then from a strong home base the gospel would spread in ever-widening circles like ripples from a stone tossed into a pool. This is still the divine principle for effective missions. The home base must be strong if it is going to support a strong foreign base.

## WHEN WE GO, WHAT DO WE SAY?

Jesus told His disciples to teach all nations. This means literally, "Make disciples of all nations." There is nothing complicated or vague about the message we are to take. Its two great parts are "repentance and remission of sins" (Luke 24:47). This is still the message. It has never changed, and never will. Sin

105

has not changed, except to grow worse. Man's basic need is still the same—to be released from sin. The passing of time does not alter these fundamentals.

The first part of the gospel message might seem negative, but it is absolutely necessary. Men must first understand that they are sinners, hopelessly lost without Christ. "All have sinned, and come short of the glory of God" (Romans 3:23). "There is none righteous, no, not one" (Romans 3:10). "The soul that sinneth, it shall die" (Ezekiel 18:4). "The wages of sin is death" (Romans 6:23).

A person will not seek a doctor's help if he does not think he is sick. Satan deceives folks into thinking they are good enough. Man has tried to eliminate "sin" from his vocabulary. Today we are told that people who do wrong are sick, not sinful. This is completely contrary to Scripture. It is a lie spread by the devil himself. Men will not call on God if they do not know they are lost and incurably sinful apart from Christ.

The second part of the message is positive, but the negative has to come first. After a man confesses his sins he is in a position to have them forgiven. This remission of sins is based solely on the atoning work of Jesus Christ on the Cross:

"Who his own self bare our sins in his own body on the tree, that we, being dead to sins, should live unto righteousness: by whose stripes ye were healed" (1 Peter 2:24). "Him hath God exalted with his right hand to be a Prince and a Saviour, for to give repentance to Israel, and forgiveness of sins" (Acts 5: 31). "Be it known unto you therefore, men and brethren, that through this man is preached unto you the forgiveness of sins" (Acts 13:38). "In whom we have redemption through his blood, the forgiveness of sins, according to the riches of his grace" (Ephesians 1:7).

## WE AREN'T GOING ALONE

"Lo, I am with you alway, even unto the end of the world" (Matthew 28:20). Those words of Jesus were addressed to His disciples just before He ascended. But they were directed to Christians of every century. This is a promise to be claimed by God's people until our Lord comes back. We are not alone!

What a wonderful story: "The Lord working with them" (Mark 16:20). How those first Christians needed His companionship! They faced a hostile world. They soon encountered fierce persecution. Church history is full of Christian martyrdoms and mistreatment. In some parts of the world God's people are suffering even today. But they have never been abandoned to face the battle alone. Jesus promised they wouldn't be.

Peter and John were arrested after a lifelong cripple was healed. The authorities had to let them go, but threatened them with warnings not to preach any more about Jesus (Acts 4:18). The response of the disciples was to go back to their own company for a great prayer meeting. The result? "And when they had prayed, the place was shaken where they were assembled together; and they were all filled with the Holy Ghost, and they spake the word of God with boldness" (Acts 4:31). The Lord lost no time in letting them know He was right beside them!

When Peter was jailed God sent an angel to deliver him (Acts 12:3-11). When Paul and Barnabas were driven out of Antioch, instead of being discouraged they were filled with joy and with the Holy Ghost (Acts 13:52). When Paul's preaching was disturbed by a demon-possessed girl he cast out the demon in the name of Jesus (Acts 16:18).

We could go on and on. The story has been the same throughout Biblical and church history. Christ has wonderfully fulfilled His promise to be with His people always.

We may not be thrown into prison or tortured for our testimony. But as long as we are in this sinful world we are in an atmosphere that is unfriendly to the gospel. We shall always encounter spiritual pressure. Satan will not stand idly by and watch us win souls without trying to interfere. One of his most effective weapons is discouragement. When he uses it on us we need to remind ourselves that we are not alone.

Jesus died to save men from sin. He will not forsake those who go forth to tell this good news. Whatever our feelings may be from day to day, His promise is as solid as a rock.


## WE'RE ALL PARTNERS

"All my prayers for you are full of praise to God! When I pray for you, my heart is full of joy, because of all your wonderful help in making known the Good News about Christ from the time you first heard it until now. And I am sure that God who began the good work within you will keep right on helping you grow in his grace until his task within you is finally finished on that day when Jesus Christ returns. How natural it is that I should feel as I do about you, for you have a very special place in my heart. We have shared together the blessings of God, both when I was in prison and when I was out, defending the truth and telling others about Christ" (Philippians 1:3-7, *Living Bible Paraphrased*).

108

That is Paul writing to the Philippian Christians. Although he was chosen by God to travel far and wide to spread the gospel, while they worked for the Lord at home, the apostle considered them his partners. Here's more:

"As you well know, when I first brought the Gospel to you and then went on my way, leaving Macedonia, only you Philippians became my partners in giving and receiving. No other church did this. Even when I was over in Thessalonica you sent help twice. But though I appreciate your gifts, what makes me happiest is the well-earned reward you will have because of your kindness" (Philippians 4:15-17, *Living Bible Paraphrased*).

Paul wanted these Christians to know he couldn't get along without them. He was physically separated from them by many miles, but they were still a part of his work. And he made it clear that they would also share in the reward.

Those who go to mission fields are partners with those who stay at home but pray and give. Every missionary will tell you he values prayer as well as financial support. So will every pastor and evangelist, and every home missionary. Those in places of spiritual leadership face battles unknown to others. They are under Satanic attack. They bear heavy responsibility. Naturally they get tired in body and in spirit. How wonderful for them to have prayer partners who are holding them up before the Lord every day. Don't forget to pray as well as give!

# 12
# *Don't Just Sit There!*

## YOU'RE AN EVANGELIST

Do those words surprise you? You thought an evangelist is a preacher who travels around the country holding revival meetings, didn't you? Well, that's *one* kind of evangelist. But if we're going to be scriptural we have to recognize that God intends for every Christian to be an evangelist.

"Evangel" means "good news." An evangelist is one who *carries* that good news. Let's never limit this job to those called to pulpit ministry. It's too much of a load to put on a few. Away with the notion that we engage a revival specialist for a week or two each year and let him do all our soul winning for us! We aren't called to be spectators. Some Christians act that way, though. They sit and watch someone else do it all while they look on as though they were viewing a TV show.

Here's what the Bible says about an evangelist who lived a long time ago:

"And the angel of the Lord spake unto Philip, saying, Arise, and go toward the south, unto the way that goeth down from Jerusalem unto Gaza, which is desert. And he arose and went: and, behold, a man of Ethiopia, a eunuch of great authority under Candace queen of the Ethiopians, who had charge of all her treasure, and had come to Jerusalem for to worship, was returning, and sitting in his chariot read Isaiah the prophet" (Acts 8:26-28).

Philip was known in the Early Church as "Philip the evangelist" (Acts 21:8). The title is a recognition of the kind of man he was. He could have been known as "Philip the deacon," for he was a deacon (Acts 6: 5). He could have been called "Philip, a man of honest report" (Acts 6:3). He might have been known as "Philip, a man full of the Holy Ghost" (Acts 6: 3). He could have been known as "Philip, a man full of wisdom" (Acts 6:3). He was all of these. But when Luke, the author of Acts, wanted to identify him he called him "Philip the evangelist." That was the best way to characterize him. He was a man obsessed with a desire to tell the good news.

Let's get this clear: Christ expects every Christian to be a witness. This is a glorious privilege; not drudgery.

## BE A LISTENER

"Then the Spirit said unto Philip, Go near, and join thyself to this chariot. And Philip ran thither to him, and heard him read the prophet Isaiah, and said, Understandest thou what thou readest? And he said, How can I, except some man should guide me? And he desired Philip that he would come up and sit with him" (Acts 8:29-31).

See how sensitive Philip was to the voice of the Holy Spirit. Just how the Spirit spoke we are not told. Probably it was by means of a deep impression in Philip's heart. It was so compelling that he knew it was not his own thought.

We, too, must learn to detect the voice of the Spirit. It's not easy in a world like ours. There's so much noise and bustle and clamor. Often the Spirit doesn't speak in loud tones. It may be only a whisper. We must train our spiritual ears to hear that whisper. This takes a lot of prayer. It also takes much time with the Bible. The Word will sharpen our spiritual senses.

The Lord leads us a step at a time. His first instructions to Philip were simply to go south toward Gaza. God seldom gives us every detail in the beginning. We must develop faith, and that means a step at a time.

Once on that Gaza highway, Philip did not know what the Lord would have him do next. He saw a chariot traveling toward Ethiopia. There was a man sitting in it, reading from a scroll. Still Philip did not know what his next move should be.

Suddenly, the Holy Spirit spoke; "Go near and join thyself to this chariot." Without such a clear command Philip certainly would not have intruded on the privacy of this government official. But when the Spirit speaks you don't have to be afraid.

Note how quick Philip was to obey, once he knew he had heard from God: "Philip ran thither to him." He still didn't know what he was supposed to do, but he was willing to let the Lord guide him. He had been commanded to come to this road, and he had come. The Holy Spirit directed him to the chariot, and he obeyed.

Sensitivity to the voice of the Holy Spirit is a quality that must be cultivated by every witness for Christ. This cannot be done if it is practiced only occasionally. We must work at it every day. We will lose valuable opportunities if we are not led by the Spirit. He knows what hearts are prepared to receive the Word. He will direct us to those individuals if we will let Him.

This important man to whom the Lord had led Philip was secretary of the treasury in Ethiopia. He was not a Jew, but in his search for truth he had gone to Jerusalem to worship. Possibly he had become an actual convert to Judaism. He was reading the Scriptures in an effort to satisfy the spiritual thirst that still nagged at him. Certainly the Holy Spirit had directed the man to the Scripture he was reading:

"The place of the Scripture which he read was this, He was led as a sheep to the slaughter; and like a lamb before his shearer, so opened he not his mouth: in his humiliation his judgment was taken away: and who shall declare his generation? for his life is taken from the earth" (Acts 8:32,33).

Obviously the eunuch was frustrated, for even after earnest study he could not comprehend what he had read. Here's how things went:

"And the eunuch answered Philip, and said, I pray thee, of whom speaketh the prophet this? of himself, or of some other man? Then Philip opened his mouth, and began at the same Scripture, and preached unto him Jesus" (Acts 8:34,35).

How fortunate that Philip knew the Scripture and could explain it to this seeker. What if he had been like some Christians today who know so little of their Bible that they can't even explain the plan of salvation?

The passage the eunuch was reading was what we now call the 53rd chapter of Isaiah. It was a prophecy of Christ. Philip understood this because he was a Christian and was taught by the Holy Spirit. Unfortunately the eunuch did not have this kind of spiritual light. He was like a man groping in the dark.

God was going to use Philip to lead him out into the light.

Notice, in verse 35, that Philip "began at the same Scripture." He based everything he said on the Word of God. He did not try to argue or advance his own theories. The Bible alone is the foundation for man's faith. The Word will speak for itself. It will not return to God void, or empty. It is like seed that needs to be sown, and when it is there will be a harvest.

Never expect to be a soul winner if you let your Bible collect dust on the shelf. It may be a beautifully bound book, but if you never open its pages it will do neither you nor anyone else any good. Don't just dwell on a few favorite passages. Get to know the whole Book, with the Holy Spirit as your teacher.

## ONE-ON-ONE

Soul winning is an individual matter. Of course, the Lord uses what we call "mass evangelism," when great crowds go to hear a preacher. Many are saved in such meetings. But this is not the only way the good news is spread. When it comes right down to basics, it's a matter of one person telling another about Christ that gets the job done.

What a great example Jesus was. Some of the greatest sermons He preached were to an audience of one. What about His sermon on the new birth? (John 3: 1-21). Jesus was talking to one man, Nicodemus, when He gave this great teaching. It was night, and the two were alone.

What about our Lord's sermon on the water of life? His congregation was one Samaritan woman (John 4: 1-26).

Jesus was never too busy with the multitudes to stop and talk to one. He was never too busy to heal one. We are born into this world as individuals, and

114

we leave it individually. We are saved the same way. The Holy Spirit comes to us as individuals and convicts us of *our* sin, not someone else's. We turn to Christ as individuals. When you win a person to the Lord you never know how many *he* may win. You may be starting a chain reaction that will bring hundreds, or even thousands, into the Kingdom.

The best way to start this one-on-one witnessing is simply to be a friend. Some people are afraid of preachers. But they aren't afraid of a friend. Lay the groundwork for your witnessing by first being a good friend. In your daily contact with your friend the Holy Spirit will turn your conversation naturally to spiritual matters. You may be surprised at the hunger your friend has in his heart to be right with God.

Timidity is no excuse for silence. Obviously not everyone is a gifted speaker. But have you ever heard a timid person get started talking about something that really interests him? Miraculously that self-consciousness seems to vanish. He gets so absorbed in what he is saying that he forgets to be timid. So let's not use the excuse, "I'm just too bashful to talk to people about Christ." If you can talk to them about the weather, or the ball game, or a TV show, you can talk to them about the most important matter of all!

Be on the lookout for opportunities to witness. Start each day with the goal in mind, "I'm going to tell at least one person about Christ before I go to bed."

## God's Love in Us

God sent His Son to this world because He "so loved the world" (John 3:16). There are many things that are hard to do unless you are motivated by love. This applies to our Christian work. Witnessing for Christ can be drudgery if we're just doing it mechan-

115

ically. It's very different when you do it out of a love for souls.

But it's not a case of developing our own natural love. It is human for us to love people that appeal to us and to whom we are attracted. When it comes to loving folks who are unlovable, this comes hard. That's where *God's* love comes in. It's what we have to have in us to overcome our human tendencies.

We must see people as God sees them. He does not dwell on their faults and bad characteristics, but on the fact that they are souls who will live somewhere forever.

Maybe we don't think enough about what it means to be lost. The worst part about it is the eternal separation from God. Hell is a place where God is eternally absent. What suffering, what agony, such a condition will produce! Men without Christ are going there. God is depending on us to keep as many of them from going as possible.

How do we get God's love inside our own hearts? By keeping as close to Him as possible. This involves a consistent prayer life. It means keeping full of His Word. It means regular worship. And it means consistency in our witnessing. If you let too much time pass without trying to win a soul, some of that love is going to slip away.

Do you remember what the Bible says about Jesus' attitude toward the rich young ruler who came to Him? Here was a fine person who had lived a good moral life. But still he was not satisfied that all was right between him and God. So he came to Jesus to find out what he must do. And listen: "Then Jesus, beholding him, loved him" (Mark 10:21). Let's pray that this can always be said of us—that when we behold lost men and women we love them.

God's love cost Him a heavy price. Real love always does. Witnessing for Christ might make it necessary sometimes to change our plans and inconvenience ourselves. We may have to go to places where we don't really want to go. But God's love in us will make it a joy, not a task that we do while chewing our fingernails in frustration. Love does make a difference! And what a reward in seeing lives that are changed because we told them of Jesus.

## START NOW!

We're supposed to be the "now" generation. But when it comes to our spiritual responsibilities we're good at crying, "Later, Lord!"

Most of us are afflicted with the disease of procrastination. We don't do today what we can put off until tomorrow. This is bad enough in secular matters, but when it gets into our Christian life it's tragic.

How long have you been telling yourself, "I'm going to witness to my neighbor," but you haven't done it yet? What if you read his obituary tomorrow and you still hadn't told him about Jesus?

The Psalmist prayed, "Remember how short my time is" (Psalm 89:47). Ours is just as short as his. The days soon turn into weeks, months, and years. The longer we put off our task of witnessing the easier it gets to let it slide. We can salve our conscience with promises of what we're going to do tomorrow. We may even get to the place that our conscience doesn't prick us as it used to.

Philip was enjoying a great revival in Samaria when the Lord called him to that desert road. There was no delay in his obedience. He didn't try to bargain with the Lord and say, "Can't You wait until a more convenient time?" When God's voice spoke,

117

"he arose and went." Is that the way we respond? It *should* be.

Every day a man lives without Christ his mind gets harder. Delay is dangerous. He may not accept Christ even when you witness to him, but your hands will be clean. You will have discharged your responsibility. If you wait until he is on a hospital bed full of tubes, needles, and sedation, he may not be able to respond. Don't let that oportunity pass. Do it now.

The time is short indeed. We are surely living in the end of this age. Jesus is coming soon. When He does, our opportunities for witnessing will be past. Our Lord himself said, "The night cometh when no man can work" (John 9:4). There is a time when opportunities abound, and there is a time when they are gone.

If we are inclined to put off our duty to witness, it is a sign we are taking it lightly. We do not sense the urgency of it. If this is the case, we had better have a prayer meeting consisting of just us and the Lord. We'd better not get off our knees until we feel an urgency that makes further delay impossible.

A lot of people won't go to church. So Christians must go to them. It's that simple!

# 13
# *Maranatha*

### IT'S A FACT

The second coming of Jesus is no myth. It's one of the clearest truths in the Bible.

First Corinthians 16:22 contains two words that are left untranslated. The verse reads, "If any man love not the Lord Jesus Christ, let him be Anathema, Maranatha." This means, "Let him be accursed. Our Lord cometh." It has been said that early Christians often greeted one another with the word, "Maranatha," meaning "Our Lord cometh." This was how earnestly they looked for Jesus to return. It was never out of their thoughts.

Jesus did not set a time for His second coming. Because He did not specify the exact time, Christians through the ages have hoped that He might come during their lifetime. They have tried to obey the Lord's warning, "Take ye heed, watch and pray: for ye know not when the time is. . . . Watch ye therefore, for ye know not when the master of the house cometh, at even, or at midnight, or at the cockcrowing, or in the morning" (Mark 13:33,35). In view of Christ's own instructions it is not wrong for us to expect Him to come in our lifetime.

The church at Thessalonica was very much interested in the Lord's return. They had acquired some mistaken ideas about it, so Paul had to give them some corrective teaching. The result was for the good of the whole church, including us. The two Thessalonian letters are full of important teaching about the end of this age. Some of the Thessalonians were worried about what might happen to Christians who died before the Lord's coming. Here is what Paul told them:

"But I would not have you to be ignorant, brethren, concerning them which are asleep, that ye sorrow not, even as others which have no hope. For if we believe that Jesus died and rose again, even so them also which sleep in Jesus will God bring with him. For this we say unto you by the word of the Lord, that we which are alive and remain unto the coming of the Lord shall not prevent [precede] them which are asleep" (1 Thessalonians 4:13-15).

This was a comfort to those Christians. It let them know that even if we die before Jesus comes back we shall not be left behind.

### "THE LORD HIMSELF"

"For the Lord himself shall descend from heaven with a shout, with the voice of the archangel, and with the trump of God" (1 Thessalonians 4:16).

When Jesus ascended to heaven, two angels suddenly stood before the watching disciples with this message: "Ye men of Galilee, why stand ye gazing up into heaven? this same Jesus, which is taken up from you into heaven, shall so come in like manner as ye have seen him go into heaven" (Acts 1:10,11). That portion of Scripture indicates two important facts about the second coming of Jesus:

1. It will be "this same Jesus." This is vital. If understood it will help us avoid a wrong view of the

120

nature of the Second Coming. It is Jesus himself who shall return. The Second Coming is not death. It is not the coming of the Holy Spirit. It was not the destruction of Jerusalem in A.D. 70 by the Romans. All of these events were quite different from the return of Jesus as the Bible describes it.

2. He will return "in like manner." His coming will be a physical one, just as His ascension was physical. His ascension was bodily; His return will also be bodily. It will be visible. The disciples watched until "a cloud received Him out of their sight" (Acts 1:9). The angel said, "Ye have seen him go into heaven" (Acts 1:11). He will also be seen at His return.

The Bible is very clear that Jesus will return personally, bodily, and visibly. Here are some more Scripture passages:

"Ye shall not see me, until the time come when ye shall say, Blessed is he that cometh in the name of the Lord" (Luke 13:35).

"And then shall they see the Son of man coming in a cloud with power and great glory" (Luke 21:27).

"We shall see him as he is" (1 John 3:2).

"For as the lightning cometh out of the east, and shineth even unto the west; so shall also the coming of the Son of man be" (Matthew 24:27).

Jesus mentioned His second coming many times prior to the night of His betrayal. The number of times He talked about it with His disciples gives some indication of its importance in the plan of God.

Some of Jesus' teaching about this great truth was in direct statements. At other times it was in parables. See Luke 12:36-40; 13:35; 17:24-36; 18:8; 19:12-27; Matthew 23:39; 24:3. Compare Matthew 24:

27 with 25:46; Mark 13:26-36; Luke 21:27-36. Base your belief on the Bible; not some human theory.

## "RAPTURE" AND "ADVENT"

The apostles also wrote about the Second Coming. James referred to it with an encouragement to patience: "Be patient therefore, brethren, unto the coming of the Lord. . . . The coming of the Lord draweth nigh" (James 5:7,8).

Peter had much to say about the Second Coming: 2 Peter 1:16; 3:3,4,10. See also 1 Peter 1:4-13; 4:13; 5:4; 2 Peter 1:6; 3:1-18.

John also wrote about the Second Coming: Revelation 22:20; 22:7,12; 3:11; 1:7; 1 John 3:2. Jude mentioned it: Jude 14. The writer of Hebrews referred to the Second Coming: Hebrews 10:37.

Paul referred to the Second Coming many times. In fact he talked about it so much that the references are too numerous to list. Among the most important are 1 Corinthians 1:8; 15:22-58; Philippians 3:20; 1 Timothy 6:14-16; 2 Timothy 4:8; Titus 2:13.

The numerous references by New Testament writers to the Second Coming are a convincing proof that they accepted it as a fact. Not only did they believe it themselves; they wanted others to believe it. That is why Paul said, "I would not have you to be ignorant, brethren" (1 Thessalonians 4:13).

The Second Coming is in two phases. First, Jesus will return for His church. This is often called "the Rapture." The word *rapture* is not in the Bible, but it means "carrying away." At the Rapture the Church will be carried away by Christ. Paul describes this in 1 Thessalonians 4:16,17:

"And the dead in Christ shall rise first. Then we which are alive and remain shall be caught up together with them in the clouds to meet the Lord in the air, and so shall we ever be with the Lord."

The second phase of Christ's coming is frequently called the "Revelation." It will occur some time after the Rapture. At that time Christ will return to the earth as King. "And his feet shall stand in that day upon the Mount of Olives, which is before Jerusalem on the east" (Zechariah 14:4). At that time Christ will establish His kingdom on the earth and rule for a millennium, or a thousand years. We believe the Church will be raptured before this millennial kingdom is established, which means that our belief is "premillennial."

All of this is literal. The resurrection of the righteous dead at the Rapture is a physical resurrection. The miraculous change of the bodies of living Christians will be physical. Jesus' return to the Mount of Olives, with His feet actually touching the earth, will be literal and physical.

### DON'T GO TO SLEEP!

"But of the times and seasons, brethren, ye have no need that I write unto you. For yourselves know perfectly that the day of the Lord so cometh as a thief in the night. For when they shall say, Peace and safety; then sudden destruction cometh upon them, as travail upon a woman with child; and they shall not escape.

"But ye, brethren, are not in darkness, that that day should overtake you as a thief. Ye are all the children of light, and the children of the day: we are not of the night, nor of darkness. Therefore let us not sleep, as do others; but let us watch and be sober. . . . For God hath not appointed us to wrath, but to obtain salvation by our Lord Jesus Christ" (1 Thessalonians 5:1-6,9).

When the disciples asked Jesus, just prior to His ascension, "Lord, wilt thou at this time restore again the kingdom to Israel?" Jesus replied, "It is not for you to know the times or the seasons, which the Father hath put in his own power" (Acts 1:6,7).

No one knows when the Lord will return. "But of that day and that hour knoweth no man, no, not the angels which are in heaven, neither the Son, but the Father" (Mark 13:32).

The important thing is not that we know *when* He will return, but *that* He will return. Believing in His coming will help keep us ready whenever it is. We will not allow the great event to find us unprepared.

Although we do not know the time of His coming, we do know that God will rapture the Church before He pours out His wrath upon the world. "For God hath not appointed us to wrath, but to obtain salvation by our Lord Jesus Christ" (1 Thessalonians 5:9).

After the Rapture the Antichrist will be revealed: "That man of sin . . . the son of perdition; who opposeth and exalteth himself above all that is called God, or that is worshiped; so that he as God sitteth in the temple of God, showing himself that he is God" (2 Thessalonians 2:3,4). This will happen after the Church has been carried away (1 Thessalonians 2:3,7,8). God will then pour out His wrath, and Christ will return to Israel "in flaming fire taking vengeance on them that know not God, and that obey not the gospel of our Lord Jesus Christ" (2 Thessalonians 1: 8). Christians will be saved from this terrible time by the Rapture.

We must not allow ourselves to become spiritually sleepy and lose our alertness concerning our Lord's return. There is too much at stake for us to grow careless. It's worth all the effort to stay awake.

## THE SIGNS ARE MULTIPLYING

Jesus forbade us to set dates for the actual day of His coming. However, He mentioned a number of signs that would indicate the time is getting close. Many Christians believe these signs are growing more numerous at this very time.

The 24th chapter of Matthew records a lengthy conversation Jesus had with His disciples about His return. They were standing close to the temple, and Jesus startled them with the prediction that that great building would one day be completely destroyed. Thinking that such a catastrophe was connected with the end of the world, the disciples asked Jesus, "When shall these things be, and what shall be the sign of thy coming, and of the end of the world?" (Matthew 24:3).

Without knowing it, the disciples actually asked Jesus about three different events: (1) "These things," meaning the destruction of the temple; (2) His coming; (3) The end of the world (age). We must read this passage carefully to know when Jesus was talking about the destruction of the temple, when He was discussing His second coming, and when He referred to the judgments at the end of the age after His feet stand on the earth again.

Jesus said there would be false christs throughout this age. He said there would also be wars and rumors of wars (Matthew 24:5,6). But just before His coming such things will intensify. Wars will not be local, but worldwide. Famines, disease epidemics, and earthquakes will be widespread. There will be not just a few false prophets, but many. A loss of faith will be commonplace (Matthew 24:7-13).

125

In Matthew 24:32,33, Jesus gave an illustration from nature: "Now learn a parable of the fig tree. When his branch is yet tender, and putteth forth leaves, ye know that summer is nigh: so likewise ye, when ye shall see all these things, know that it is near, even at the doors."

The New Testament writers mentioned many more signs of our Lord's return. Paul told Timothy that in the last days "perilous times shall come" (2 Timothy 3:1). He then proceeded to describe the nature of much of the human race at the end of this age (2 Timothy 3:2-7). It is a picture of total moral and spiritual degradation.

Jesus said that world conditions before His coming will be comparable to those in the days of Noah (Matthew 24:37-39). If you want to know what those days were like, read Genesis 6:5-7. It certainly sounds like the days we're living in right now.

## THE BLESSED HOPE

Christians have looked for the second coming of Christ ever since He went back to heaven. Paul calls it the church's "blessed hope" (Titus 2:13).

Of course it is not a blessed hope to those who are not prepared. Quite the contrary. It frightens them. Only those who are truly converted will be raptured. The man who rejects Christ has nothing to look forward to but the wrath of God.

If Jesus did not come back there would be no end to the present state of affairs. The world is in a frightful condition. Injustice, lawlessness, immorality, and selfishness have the human race in a death grip. Would you like to think that such things will never be straightened out?

History is actually "His story." World events are not moving along haphazardly. Every day is like a piece in a puzzle that God himself is fitting together. The Lord is very much in control. He is allowing man to have his day. But that day is coming to an end.

The Bible does not teach that the world will get better and better until the kingdom of God is finally established on earth by man's own efforts. The Bible makes it clear that the world will get worse and worse until God has to intervene supernaturally. Could the Word be any plainer than this:

"And to you who are troubled rest with us, when the Lord Jesus shall be revealed from heaven with his mighty angels, in flaming fire taking vengeance on them that know not God, and that obey not the gospel of our Lord Jesus Christ: who shall be punished with everlasting destruction from the presence of the Lord, and from the glory of his power; when he shall come to be glorified in his saints, and to be admired in all them that believe" (2 Thessalonians 1:7-10).

Until Jesus comes, even Christians will be subject to sickness, sorrow, pain, and death. His return will end these things for His true followers. The trials of earth will be over and forgotten. The faithful will receive their rewards at last (2 Corinthians 5:10; 1 Corinthians 3:11-15; Revelation 22:12).

After Jesus had told His disciples about some of the signs of His coming He said, "And when these things begin to come to pass, then look up and lift up your heads, for your redemption draweth nigh" (Luke 21:28). Don't look down. Look up! That's where our deliverance is coming from. What a hope! No wonder Paul called it "blessed."